Discipline Me RIGHT

Tips *from* Teens *for* Parents

MARY SIMMONS *with* BERT SIMMONS

Tips *from* Teens *for* Parents

MARY SIMMONS *with* BERT SIMMONS

Horizon
Springville, Utah

Dedicated to my parents
and to my students,
for all you have taught me

ISBN 13: 978-0-88290-962-2
Published by Horizon, an imprint of Cedar Fort, Inc., 2373 W. 700 S., Springville, UT 84663
Distributed by Cedar Fort, Inc., www.cedarfort.com

Library of Congress Cataloging-in-Publication Data

Simmons, Mary, 1955-
  Discipline me right / Mary Simmons, with Bert Simmons.
    p. cm.
  Includes bibliographical references.
  ISBN 978-0-88290-962-2 (acid-free paper)
  1. Discipline of children. 2. Parenting. 3. Parent and child. I.
Simmons, Bert, 1935- II. Title.
  HQ770.4.S56 2009
  649'.64--dc22
                                    2009009814

Cover design by Angela D. Olsen
Cover design © 2008 by Lyle Mortimer
Edited and typeset by Heidi Doxey

Printed in the United States of America

10 9 8 7 6 5 4 3 2 1

Printed on acid-free paper

This book is a *must* read for every parent! Parents who use these excellent behavior management skills will find that they will build trust, respect, and self discipline in their children. In my twenty-nine years of educating high school students, I learned that students want rules and limits, even though they will test them all the way! This book will help parents learn how to successfully enforce the rules and limits and still show their child love and respect! Isn't it worth taking the time to discipline correctly in order to have a child grow up to be a successful adult who in turn returns the respect, love, and trust that you showed them?

Glenna R. Cannon
Superintendent, Pioneer Career and Technology Center

Discipline Me Right is a must read for every parent, teacher and administrator. If you have children, plan to have children, teach children, or work with children in any capacity, this book is for you. As a former principal at the elementary, middle and high school levels, I am thrilled that Mary Simmons has taken the time to write this informative book. The practicality of *Discipline Me Right* is absolutely astounding. This book is straightforward and realistic.

Young developing adults and children want and need parameters as well as consistent and fair disciplining. Without a doubt, this author has done an outstanding job of identifying key issues that parents and educators face on a daily basis. Most important, she has outlined techniques and strategies that can be effectively applied by parents, teachers, administrators, and others who have been charged to work with, nurture, educate, and raise children. Once again, I say to you, *Discipline Me Right* is an absolute must read.

Dr. Joyce M. Gray
President & Owner, Jam G Consulting, Incorporated
President, Utah Alliance of Black School Educators

Acknowledgments

I would like to thank my father, Bert Simmons and his wife, Betty Jo, for their inspiration, ideas, skills, and input, without which *Discipline Me Right* would not exist. Thanks also to everyone in my family who encouraged me, particularly my sister, Sandy, and my mother, Esther, who have always believed in me and my writing.

Thanks to Cedar Fort Inc. and to Ted and Liz Freemantle for their support when I was writing this book on a wing and a prayer. Thanks also to the administration of Bothell High School, particularly Donna Tyo who served many of us as a disciplinary role model.

I am deeply indebted to the authors I used as sources, whose wisdom and analysis transcend my own in so many ways, and to my students who lent their voices to this project.

Thank you to my friends and family whose belief in this project sometimes went beyond my own: Ken and Joe Symanski, Kim Glandon, Kathleen Flatness, Candia Sanders, Tracy Herrold, Aimee Misovich, and Kathy Phoutrides. Your support has meant more than you know.

With fond and wistful thanks, I remember Ginger Chadwick, who didn't smile at her students "until Christmas" but started squirt gun fights with them in May. I owe her so much. My deepest and most profound gratitude is to God who fills my life with opportunity and whose blessing I wish for everyone who holds this book.

Contents

Preface

The 1st Commandment: Discipline Your Kids Right!

I am an English teacher and parent. For five years, I asked my high school seniors, about five hundred of them, to write "Ten Commandments for Parents" when we studied the novel *Ordinary People* by Judith Guest. This exercise got them thinking about the important theme of parenting in the novel and the very real prospect of their own future parenthood. This is what I said to them: "You aren't parents yet, but most of you will be one day. Think about it: Even though you aren't parents, you're experts. You've been observing your parents for eighteen years now, and you know what works and what doesn't." At first, it was just for fun and to get the wheels turning in their heads. It turned into a lot more.

Eventually, I typed up and tallied their commandments, thousands of them, and discovered a clearly ranked and impressive set of directives:

1. Discipline Me Right
2. Provide for Me Well
3. Allow Me Freedom
4. Be a Role Model
5. Be There
6. Respect My Individuality
7. Respect My Privacy
8. Love Me
9. Don't Embarrass Me
10. Have Reasonable Expectations

These commandments, to a degree, reflect an advanced stage of childhood. After all, at seventeen and eighteen, my seniors were approaching adulthood, and quite concerned about autonomy and freedoms and being treated with respect. However, as you will see, their commandments, with few exceptions, mirror what educators, child psychologists, and the wise and seasoned have been saying for ages: Kids *need* positive discipline (number one), support, freedom, role models, their parent's presence and attention, respect, privacy, love, and expectations—and they need them in that order, according to the numbers. Love is not number one; it's number eight. Love isn't all you need. First and foremost, a child needs behavioral parameters. He must be *taught* how to respect others and cooperate within society. It will not happen through osmosis.

However, in many American households, the most important job in the world isn't being done. Kids are being raised on electronics: iPods, cell phones, TV, the Internet, and video games that regularly depict cold-blooded violence. Most of the contact that kids have with adults is spent with people who are not their parents. These people may or may not take an interest in them: bus drivers, daycare providers, babysitters, nannies, teachers, coaches, and bosses. The role models kids see on TV and in the movies are often crass, heartless, and brainless, while on the Internet they observe the anything-can-be-posted antics of MySpace and YouTube. In addition, porn is ever accessible, where people's bodies are objects to be used, not unlike the targets for shooters in the video games kids play.

The message? "People are expendable; they don't matter that much, and neither do you, kid." When did the media start raising our kids? Why are some people not raising their own kids, and how did that get to be okay?

The result of this lack of direction, limits, and discipline are children who, in spite of the cult of self-esteem boosting in recent years, feel truly inadequate, insecure, and under-loved. These kids are frustrated and they show it in a variety of ways:

1. disrespect toward parents, including disobedience, mouthing off, insults, stealing, and physical and mental abuse
2. illegal drug use, alcohol use, and prescription drug abuse
3. cutting, anorexia, bulimia, and suicide (They attack not just themselves but others via MySpace and other internet venues. They bully others through gossip via cell phones and text messages, or direct verbal and physical fighting.)

4. rebellious, experimental sexual activity resulting in a record number of pregnancies and abortions, not to mention the psychological ramifications of promiscuity

5. disobedience and disrespect toward other authority figures such as their teachers, making teaching, as a profession, even more difficult than it already is and contributing to an alarming attrition rate among new teachers (In a very direct way, our children's misbehavior is contributing to the education crisis in this country; 50 percent of all new teachers quit in the first five years.)

Many parents do not know what to do with their kids. In America, we have clueless parents, parents who sort of get it, and a very tiny percentage of parents who know how to discipline their kids in any situation. We all want to be in the last category.

When I saw that my students' first commandment had to do with the right way to discipline kids, I knew I had to talk to my dad about writing a book. My father, Bert Simmons, a former teacher and principal and now an educational consultant with his own company, Simmons Associates, The Education Company, offers schools around the country a "comprehensive behavior management system." In other words, he's a discipline expert. What I've always loved about his approach to education and discipline, and which I appreciate even more now that I'm a teacher, is the accessibility of his technique. Bert Simmons is practical and aims at the solution, and his methods work. He is warm and approachable, but he is also no-nonsense. I knew his years of experience and the specific techniques he had honed in his business and as a parent of five would benefit parents struggling with similar issues. I have used his techniques as a parent and in my own classroom with great success. The skills Bert teaches nurture our personal boundaries and sense of authority.

That is where this book comes in. Never before have these techniques, and the philosophy behind them, been more needed. His approach is not complicated. With a few core skills, a confident mindset, and a plan—all of which are contained in this book—you can become the parent your child so desperately needs.

From his work in schools as a teacher, administrator, and discipline consultant over the last fifty years, my father estimates that parents without a clue make up about 40 percent of the parents in the United States. That means 4 out of 10 parents do not know what to do with their kids. Period.

Clueless parents tend to be passive and permissive (doing nothing)—or overtly hostile (yelling, screaming, and physically abusing) toward their children. There's a right way and a wrong way to discipline kids.

It's true that some parents don't care about their parenting role at all, but most parents *do* care; they want to get it right, but they don't know how. Most of that clueless 40 percent hope that just loving their kids will make up for any parental mistakes they make. They figure their kids will turn out okay, in spite of the fact that they have used weak discipline tactics—or no discipline at all! But the kids do not turn out okay. Discipline is such an important need that, if untended or withheld, the child becomes angry and feels deprived. Every year, society absorbs more and more angry, alienated youth as a direct result of their parents' lack of skill.

Are intentions enough? Is love enough? We see kids from age two to twenty-two disrespecting their parents in public on a regular basis: kids screaming in the grocery store, sullen teens using four-letter words with their parents, little kids pulling on their parents, parents pulling on their kids, kids hitting their parents, parents hitting their kids. If you're a teacher, you have to deal with the learned disrespect many kids bring from home. All of us have been served by teens in stores and restaurants who don't know how to say "thank you," who don't think the rules apply to them, or who have no concept of respecting their elders. Maybe at one time we thought love was enough. The Beatles idealistic song, "All You Need Is Love," still runs in our veins from the 1960s. But parenting, the down and dirty day-to-day drill of raising our kids, tells us otherwise. Love *isn't* all you need. Discipline must come first. You need a few simple skills, and that is why you need this book.

Even if you are one of the approximately 60 percent of parents who have a fair-to-good idea of what you should do with your kids *most* of the time, you still need some solid know-how for the tough times, and the tough times will come. I guarantee it.

Here's the irony: The very kids who sabotage parents and teachers on a daily basis—the teenagers who argue with us, test us, challenge our authority, beg us for things, don't do their homework, attempt to make us feel guilty, sneak out at night to engage in risky activities, yell, cry, and act in seemingly irrational ways—are the same kids who *know* what they need from us adults, and the first teen commandment—"discipline me right"—shows that.

Kids know instinctively what they need from their parents. However, they don't always know *consciously* what they need or recognize when a need is being met—nor do they necessarily *like it* when it's being met, especially if it runs counter to their own will. Kids may know exactly what they need from their parents, but they don't always know what the meeting of a need is supposed to look like. Neither do many parents. In this book, you will see the wisdom stirring in the young and learn to balance it with the skills and experience of age.

The same admonitions came up again and again. Therefore, it is interesting to note which concerns came up the most, and it is essential to address each of them in the order of their importance. Each section in this book is a subtopic of that first commandment. At the beginning of each chapter you will see the words: "This is what the kids say," and after, "This is how to interpret it." That is because effective, assertive, proactive parents know that kids have good instincts but as developing creatures they do not possess full knowledge. Knowing how to interpret what our kids say is essential to a balanced adult perspective.

Discipline must come first so that love can happen. Parents get into trouble when they think of "love" as simple affection—the warm, nurturing feelings we have toward our young. Remember that "love" ended up as number eight on my students' top ten commandment list. The thing to remember is that discipline *is* a form of love. Love indeed underlies every positive parental act. It's just that sometimes love requires us to do the difficult thing. It requires courage. Love requires us not only to hug our kids and offer them sweet reassurance but to be tough, and to speak and act in ways that cause discomfort. The first commandment, discipline, is love in action—love going to work. This isn't fuzzy love. This isn't love as generalized in platitudes like, "love is all you need." This isn't lazy love, and it isn't politically correct.

So we have to change our thinking. Political correctness is based on the concept of democracy and equal power, which has no place in the family unit. One of the original goals of political correctness was to provide a minimum of offense, usually to racial, cultural, or identity groups. That's great. However, political correctness has inappropriately seeped into the American family. Many parents are afraid of offending; they're afraid to be the bad guy. They're afraid of coming off as mean and insensitive; they are afraid of being judged. They are afraid they will come across as oppressive, even abusive, if they wield their parental power, so they back out of their role of authority, at home and in public. That is exactly what has happened in too many households: Kids are in charge because parents are afraid. Sounds ridiculous, doesn't it? Read on.

Now, we all assume that political correctness originated with the intention of including and accepting all cultures and identities—a noble cause. It was also an attempt to treat all people well and help the underprivileged—another worthy cause. However, the marriage of political correctness with the legal system has created a culture of fear. The original intention of overturning oppression has been replaced by fear of legal reprisal. If you don't talk, act, or treat people in a certain way, you could be in a lot of trouble. You could be sued. People are now generally afraid to speak their minds or appear politically incorrect, which has a paralyzing effect on freedom of speech and action in this country. It has also made people afraid to take charge of raising their own children.

In addition, political correctness focuses on victims and what they deserve for compensation. This runs counter to the belief that all people should take responsibility for their lives, regardless of circumstance. This is not to say that real victims shouldn't be compensated and helped, but we all know that the true aim of helping the oppressed has been distorted and the system milked by those who stand to gain by litigation. The victim mentality of political correctness runs counter to healthy family life.

Euphemisms have also played a part in altering family life. These days, especially in education, there is a euphemism for everything—all unacceptable behavior can be either excused or neatly labeled. Teachers are used to parents making excuses for their kids: "Johnny has ADD; that's why he can't do his homework." When, really, Johnny is allowed to stay up as long he likes playing video games. No one has an attention span or work ethic after only a couple hours of sleep. And here's my personal favorite, "Gina has Oppositional Defiance Disorder (ODD); that's why she shouts at her teachers and isn't afraid to cause a scene." When, really, Gina has been deprived of discipline her entire life and has, therefore, developed no self-control.

We all know excuse-making is called *enabling*. What I and some other child advocates want to make clear is the effect this politically correct mindset is having on the raising of our children. We need to tell the truth, stop the excuses, and take charge of our families. With political correctness, every situation is a democracy. Everyone is entitled to equal rights. This is an appropriate sentiment in politics but not in families. In recent years, educators have been asked to consider "the democratic classroom," where children are encouraged to have a voice and make choices where their education is concerned. While this can be beneficial in certain, limited situations, the wisdom and authority of the teacher should never be compromised by the immaturity of youth. Would you really want your child to design the curriculum? I think not, and yet you wouldn't mind if their constructive ideas were heard and considered by the teacher. The same applies to parenting. A child should be able to approach a trusted parent and have constructive input into the functioning of the household, but the parent's authority—as long as he is a healthy, loving adult—should never be compromised or overridden by the will of the child. The politicizing of the family unit results in these beliefs:

- A child should have equal rights (equal to the parent); the family is a democracy.
- A child can be reasoned with from the earliest years.
- A child's sense of right and wrong can be appealed to from the earliest years.
- Any kind of corporal punishment is child abuse.
- A parent should never express frustration or anger but always speak in calm, measured tones.
- Parents who do not allow their willful and high-spirited children to have their way are squelching creativity and expression.
- A child should be advocated for, protected, and excused from wrong-doing since finding fault causes guilt and other negative emotions.
- A child can be fit into any adult career plan, no matter how time-consuming.
- Always consult the experts because they always know best.

The belief that young people are miniature adults with the rights and privileges thereof is absurd. Young people are developing creatures who need assistance, mentoring, guidance and discipline from adults.

Politically correct people believe that it is improper to offend others, but children *must* be offended in order to grow up and develop properly! They don't know better yet! Politically correct people believe that every controversy or struggle is about the dispensing of power, control, force, and compulsion, and it may be, but this kind of political discussion shouldn't even happen in the realm of the family: It is not a democracy, nor should it be. A healthy family is a loving autocracy with clear rights and boundaries affecting all members.

Politically *in*correct parenting is the alternative, then, and it is not for the lazy or irresponsible. Go ahead and take away the crayons when it's bedtime; you won't be squelching creativity. Don't allow your child to speak disrespectfully to you; you won't be squelching his sense of expression. It's time for you to listen to yourself and your best instincts, and it's time to listen to the big kids—the teenagers—whose input informs this book. They are the ones who are old enough to look back and reflect on the best and worst parenting practices.

What I love about teenagers is their humor, spontaneity, and precocious wisdom. I am continually surprised and delighted by the hilarious things they say, the uncanny insights they bring to the study of literature, and their ability to "keep it real." If nothing else, teenagers are in search of personal truth. Every teenager is on a quest to define himself—a self apart from his parents, siblings, friends, and the collective "them" they have come to know. Teenagers, like all kids, are in a continual state of *becoming*. They are on a journey with more choices—and more pressures—than any of us have ever known. At their particular time of life, when their mood and persona can change from moment to moment, they appreciate honesty in others, want to be honest themselves, and appreciate the consistency and dependability of adults who are committed to caring about them. They need us, you see, because they are still kids.

Teens may *look* nearly like adults and even act mature some of the time, but even the most mature, responsible kid doesn't always act mature or responsible all the time, and that is not a bad thing. One of my senior girls, for example, an A student who held down a 20-hour-a-week job during her senior year, served on several student committees, and had the run of the school because administrators trusted her implicitly, still showed me on occasion that she was a kid. After school one day, she stayed after to talk. I was shuffling through my desk looking for something, talking but not watching, when I finally looked up to find her walking on top of the desks, idly carrying on the conversation, stepping from one desk to another, as though she were a fairy princess and the desks were lily pads. That's not something an adult would do; it was more like something a six-year-old would do on an especially challenging curb or park bench. Even though she was 18 and would be ranked among the most mature of her class, she was still, obviously and endearingly, a kid.

The difficulty lies in remembering that these young men and women, poised on the threshold of adulthood, capable of assuming *some* adult responsibility, possessing the power to create life and also to take it, are still kids in a very real way. They need responsibility and respect; they deserve the chance to make mistakes and grow on their own. At the same time, they need firm adult presences in their lives. Big kids, just like the little ones, still require discipline, financial support, a safe and stable environment, and moral direction in a culture that seems bent on destroying them and the parent-child relationship. My hope is that the wonderful teenagers I teach will take their own advice and raise their children assertively and attentively. It is my great hope that people who are already parents will take my seniors' first commandment to heart and change the course of a nation.

When you decide to be a parent, you are taking a giant leap of faith. In spite of electronic entertainment that promises to shorten your child's attention span and reduce his literacy, in spite of salacious sexuality in the media, in spite of the horrendous violence your child will absorb in video games, movies, and on the evening news, in spite of a materialistic mindset that causes many parents to spend more and more time away from their kids to earn more money and buy more things, in spite of all this, you must believe that, somehow, in toxic twenty-first-century America, your child can grow into a loving, well-mannered, empathetic, successful adult.

And you are right. But you are only right if you realize that you, as a parent, play the most important role in your child's life—period. You can pull off this minor miracle if and only if you are willing to take the necessary steps and make the necessary choices that this all important-role requires.

This book will provide skills to heal the parent-child bond, which is under attack in this culture, and how you, with the advice of my students and Bert Simmons, can reclaim the sacred trust between you and your child. After all, you want your child to grow up to be a mensch, "a human being with compassion, commitment, courage, a person whose life is guided by a core of strength and a code of fairness." As child therapist Haim Ginott explained back in the 1960s, "To achieve these humane goals, we need humane methods. Love is not enough. Insight is insufficient. Good parenting takes skill."[1]

Perhaps we can take a cue from folks in the Himalayas. According to a recent *Seattle Times* article, "The tiny Himalayan village of Bhutan long ago dispensed with the notion of Gross National Product as a gauge of well-being. The king decreed that his people would aspire to Gross National Happiness instead."[2] In this book, we will look at what truly makes parents and children happy. With skills and positive authority, we can aspire to and attain true happiness and restore parenthood to the joy it was meant to be.

As an aside, teachers hear the same stories again and again—only the details change. Therefore, the people and circumstances portrayed in this book could be composite in nature or sound very much like other people and situations. All names are fictional except for those of individuals who gave permission for their names to be used. I have taken care to preserve the privacy of all real persons, and the resemblance of any composite character to any actual person is entirely coincidental.

Notes:

1. Haim Ginott, *Between Parent and Teenager* (New York University: The Macmillan Company, 1969), 243.
2. "How happy are we? Danes are an 8.2, but Americans only a 7.4," Sterling, Associated Press via Seattle Times online: http://seattletimes.nwsource.com/html/nationworld/2003855122_happy27.html.

Introduction

Parents are the most powerful determiner of a child's well-being. The parent is the single most important influence in a child's life. This occurs with effective as well as ineffective parents—for good or for bad. The kind of adults we grow up to be is determined by our childhood experiences. Child psychologist Robert Shaw calls the mother-child relationship, "incredible," "absolutely unique," and "the single most sacred thing in our culture."[1] In his best-selling book, *The Seat of the Soul*, Gary Zukav unequivocally describes the importance of parenthood: "Your parents are the souls to whom you are closest in your lifetime, and whose influence upon you is the greatest."[2] This doesn't mean that we should blame our parents for what is wrong in our lives, nor does it mean that people can't rise above unfortunate childhood circumstances, nor does it mean that parents should worry about being perfect. The problem lies in the belief that the parent-child bond is not as important as it once was. This clearly affects the way we discipline—or don't discipline—our kids.

In *From Risk to Resilience*, educator and consultant E. Timothy Burns reminds us that the world has changed dramatically in the last 50 years, affecting both education and the way we raise our children. Fifty years ago, parenting and teaching were not politically correct. Prior to 1963, Burns points out, each American graduating class showed improvement in the areas of discipline, motivation, achievement, and comprehension. In other words, "young people's ability to step into an adult world as competent, relatively integrated adult figures" seems to have gotten better with every passing year—until 1963.[3] What happened in 1963? The Kennedy assassination happened in front of our eyes, drug use increased among the young, and TV had become an undisputable member of the family.

By 1963, the media was touching our lives in an unprecedented fashion. We had also moved from a primarily agrarian society, where families and neighbors lived and worked together closely and interdependently, to a society where 90 percent of us lived in urban and suburban settings. Where once relatives, neighbors, and the larger community provided a "safety net" for children, this new decline in community reduced the number of adults a child could depend on for recognition and support.[4]

Children used to spend far more time with their parents—and receive more discipline than they do now. Burns cites E. Stephen Glenn when he points out that a child in the 1930s spent three to four hours a day interacting with her family, while, in the 1990s, the average middle-class child spent about twelve and half *minutes* a day with her father.[5] If parents are the most important people in their kids' lives, how did it become okay to check in for just a few minutes a day?

Burns acknowledges that in the 1970s the Carter administration tried to address the symptoms of lower achievement and declining quality of life among youth—teen pregnancy, suicide, alcohol and drug abuse, low self-esteem, and runaways. They funneled money into programs and agencies to rehabilitate youth, but things just continued to get worse.[6] What we have to admit is that these problems, these symptoms, cannot be fixed with government. They can only be healed through the institution of the family and the parent-child relationship.

In America, we now have the largest population of disconnected and disaffected youth in history, but kids can't be rehabilitated if they were never *habilitated*—raised to be fit and healthy within the norms and expectations of civilized society—in the first place! Every year, teachers see a greater lack of civil and appropriate behavior in their classrooms. According to Burns, this is due to unmet developmental needs in the child and to increasing environmental stress.[7] Many parents are not even providing the minimum attention their child needs. Kids have been released into a pernicious popular culture that feeds on their vulnerability and appeals to the lowest common denominator of human behavior.

The result is that more of our kids than ever suffer from *alienation*, a lack of bonding and belonging, and *anomie*, or simply not knowing what is healthy and normal. E. Timothy Burns borrowed these terms from psychologist Urie Bronfenbrenner, and they are important to remember:

> **Alienation**—"a lack of certain essential conditions for human health. These are a lack of connectedness, a lack of bonding and/or a lack of belonging."[8]
>
> **Anomie**—"refers to 'normlessness'—not knowing what normal is. Those brought up not knowing what normal is, are growing up in a culture with no structure. For most of us, 'normal' means a culture which has more or less clear values and consistent sanctions on what shouldn't

be done, coupled with rewards and encouragement for what should be done." In addition, anomie describes a condition that is characterized by a lack of coping skills that allow us to deal successfully with stress.[9]

Kids like this have not been taught correct behavior. They have not been disciplined. Correct behavior must be taught. But there is a right way and a wrong way to discipline. For instance, we know that blowing up at our kids is wrong, but we also need to realize that too much patience is wrong, too. Parents within the politically correct parenting model are not allowed to get upset at their kids or take charge. A politically correct parent is not allowed to express frustration or anger because it may damage the child's fragile psyche.

In his excellent book, *The Epidemic: The Rot of American Culture, Absentee and Permissive Parenting, and the Resultant Plague of Joyless, Selfish Children*, child psychologist Robert Shaw reminds us of a scene we have all witnessed—the parent who *asks* a misbehaving child in public to stop her behavior, with a voice that rises in "that politically correct, measured sound"—instead of taking charge and demanding the child stop *now*. The child then throws a tantrum and must be dragged out of the store. Shaw points out that such a child is "literally being tortured by his mother's indecisiveness."[10]

Small children do not possess a solid moral foundation, the will to do the right thing because it is the right thing to do, until age seven.[11] That's a long time to be talking sense, reason, and right and wrong to a little kid before she actually understands the difference. That gives her plenty of time, while you're being patient and politically correct, to take charge and override that family democracy.

TAKING CHARGE

So what does taking charge look like? Here is a technique, in my father's own words, that he has taught thousands of parents:

> Children need to be reminded who is in charge. There comes a time when a child literally needs to be asked, "Who is your mother?"
> "Well, you're my mother," the child will say.
> "Who's in charge here?"
> "You're in charge."
> There's a time when this needs to happen.
> "Who's your father?"

"You're my father."

"Who's in charge? Is it you or is it me?"

If you have a really oppositional kid, the kid will indicate that he is in charge, and the conversation may go like this:

"Well, it's me," she'll say. "I'm in charge of my own life."

"True, but who is in charge of this family?"

"Well, you aren't being fair . . . " "Time-out," you say. "Who's your father?"

There's a time when this parental role has to be defined. With an oppositional kid, clarification of the parental role will come late because it wasn't properly established in early childhood. People with oppositional kids will be playing catch-up in middle school or high school. The kid will start to push, push, push, because the parent's authority wasn't established early on, but it can still be done.

Parents who have already established positive authority (and, therefore, trust and bonding) will have a much easier time, but even cooperative kids need to be reminded who's in charge on occasion.

Taking charge means saying what you mean, meaning what you say, and never saying anything to a child that you cannot back up.

Commandment #1—Discipline Me Right

This is the number one commandment my seniors wrote more often than any other. It has been said that the way a parent disciplines a child sets the tone for the entire parent-child relationship and determines critical aspects of the developing child's psychological makeup. Consciously or unconsciously, kids apparently know this. In this commandment and its subtopics, you will see complaints and commendations for parents at their worst—and best—moments in this twenty-four-hour job.

As I mentioned earlier, *Discipline Me Right* has been divided into subtopics according to the numbers. The most prevalent will be listed first and so on. To the best of my ability, I have paraphrased the words of my students in the subtopics and provided commentary and skills for parents under each subtopic in the text of the book. You can view a complete list of the commandments my students wrote in Appendix C.

Subtopics

1. Be fair and compromising. Be flexible, reasonable, forgiving, and

understanding. Be a thoughtful and calm referee, advisor, and teacher.

2. Do not overreact and resort to irrational, ineffective behaviors like yelling and hitting or assigning arbitrary punishments that may be disproportionate to the offense.

3. Do not abuse me; do not misuse your power as the adult or misuse me, physically or verbally.

4. Do not manipulate, force (coerce), assume the worst of me, or play mean mind games in an attempt to control me.

5. Enforce the rules, keep me in line, hold me accountable, hold me responsible. Use tough love if necessary.

6. Do not revoke my privileges and don't ground me (because it doesn't work).

7. Set rules, limits, and boundaries but make them reasonable.

8. Respect me, and do not allow disrespect toward yourself. Show that you trust me. Never give up on me. Reward and praise good behavior.

9. Let me handle my own issues, including my own mistakes. Do not pester, nag, lecture, or hassle your teen about things he or she needs to do or did wrong.

What do you do when your child defies you? How do you react when your child does something to make you angry? What does your body say? How does your voice sound? How does your face look? How do you set limits and boundaries, and what do you do when you're pushed? Let's talk about parenting styles.

PARENTING STYLES IN *ORDINARY PEOPLE*

Ordinary People by Judith Guest, the novel that inspired my seniors to think about parenting, provides several parenting styles to observe: the worried "helicopter parent," the ice queen, the cynical been-there-done-that father, the parent figure who embraces then rejects, absent parents, the laid-back mom who isn't afraid not to be perfect, and the positive parent stand-in—the one healthy adult who makes all the difference in the life of a needy child. You may remember the 1980 film directed by Robert Redford and starring Donald Sutherland, Mary Tyler Moore, Judd Hirsch, and Timothy Hutton.

The story focuses on seventeen-year-old Conrad after he tries to commit suicide. His elder and more perfect brother, Buck, drowned in a boating accident the year before, so Conrad gets to deal with survivor's guilt, his mother's rejection, the grief of his parents, his own grief, and the repercussions of his suicide attempt. Sounds like depressing stuff, but *Ordinary People* gets more life-affirming as it goes. Conrad endures and rises above his mother's icy rejection as he is given the opportunity to heal emotionally through the support of his father and his psychiatrist, Dr. Berger.

The parenting styles of Beth and Cal, Conrad's parents, are in stark contrast throughout the book. While Beth's perfectionist, rigid, and judgmental expectations wither Conrad's already shaky self-image, Cal's constant hovering (the typical "helicopter parent") threatens to smother Conrad altogether. Once Cal lightens up and learns to trust his son's coping skills, and once Cal gets in touch with his own issues of abandonment and inadequacy, he is able to release Conrad from his anxious clutches and allow him the freedom he needs. As a result, Conrad blossoms and grows.

However, the character who provides the best example of parenting in the book isn't Conrad's parent at all. It is Dr. Berger, played by Judd Hirsh in the movie, who is able to hold Conrad accountable for his actions and feelings, while Conrad's real father enters his own healing process and reclaims his parental authority. Dr. Berger can even be said to discipline Conrad, when he insists upon the truth at all times. He is tough and loving. He is the one healthy adult who pulls Conrad through his crisis.

Conrad's mother, Beth, is cold and detached. When she does react, she tends to overreact. She manipulates, accuses, shouts, and abuses; she can turn on a dime from ice queen to drama queen. She represents, in my seniors' first commandment, the negative disciplinarian.

On the other hand, Cal cares but is ineffective as a disciplinarian until the end. In the last few pages of the book, Cal, for the first time in the book, gets really angry at his son. Conrad makes a flippant, disrespectful remark, and Cal snaps at him and puts him in his place. A stunned Conrad has been reminded who is in charge and instantly apologizes, and actually asks for more discipline. "Haul my ass a little, tell me to shape up," he says.[12]

This is the note the book ends on. The father has regained his authority and the son senses boundaries and a new direction from a more mature, in-charge father.

ASSERTIVE, NONASSERTIVE, AND HOSTILE PARENTS

According to Bert Simmons, there are three types of parents: assertive, non-assertive, and hostile. He coaches teachers, principals, and parents in school districts across the U.S. to be positive and assertive with kids. The specific skills he teaches are explained later on in this book. First, it's important to understand the differences between nonassertive and assertive parents.

Nonassertive and Hostile

The reason why people get into so much difficulty in their interactions, according to Bert, is that "the overwhelming majority of the population is nonassertive and hostile in their actions. They do not take assertive, positive action, and then when things get tough, they get mad."

- Most people are habitually nonassertive which usually culminates in hostility. This can produce domestic violence, for instance.
- This kind of emotional and physical violence results from a combination of nonassertive behavior (not acting), allowing a negative situation to go on and on, and then reacting with anger and hostility at a later point.
- People who don't know how to handle anger become hostile.

Assertive and Proactive

Bert points out that only "about 5 percent of the population operates at a higher level, at a proactive, assertive level. These are hopefully our leaders, and our really good parents." This percentage can go way up, with awareness and parents taking positive action.

- Proactive, assertive people think ahead.
- They conduct themselves in an assertive manner, meaning they get their needs met, but they don't do it at the expense of others.
- They are firm, fair, and consistent.
- Assertive people get their needs met as a parent in appropriate ways that are uncharacteristic of most of the population.

As Bert says,

> Most people will waffle. They will have no backbone; they will have no concentration on their role. But if you're assertive, you will be firm, and your kids will know the rules of the road. If you're not assertive, you're passive, wishy-washy, you hear no evil, and, as a result, your

parenting will be very weak. This kind of parent always wants to be a child's friend. They don't want to discipline their children. They just want to love them. As a result, those parents live a life of pain.

Assertive people are positive; they have a smile on their face. They don't raise their voice. They don't call people names. They say what they mean; they mean what they say. According to Bert, they go by a personal oath based on mutual respect:

Parent Creed
As a parent I cannot allow my child to do anything that is not in his or her best interest—or mine.

Assertive parents have a guide for what is acceptable and not acceptable. They live their creed on a daily basis. The assertive parent is totally aware of his child's need for assertive authority at all times; it's what his life is all about.

Discipline is an act of courage and love

Discipline is an act of love, for your child and for yourself. The father in *Ordinary People*, Cal, a man who grew up an orphan with few role models, does not think he deserves to be angry or in charge. At the end of the book, when he stands up for himself to his petulant, demanding son, we see a man who has finally grown into his role, and we see Conrad respond accordingly. Conrad is sincerely shocked, in a good way; he apologizes for being disrespectful, and then encourages his dad to keep it up.

Cal has stopped being chicken. In *Chicken Parents, Chicken Schools*, authors Roland and Sherry Wong say, "In a nutshell, today's parents are afraid."[13] They are afraid to be the bad guy, the authority figure, "preferring the far easier and apparently more palatable role of buddy or best friend."[14] But our kids want us to be the authorities. They need us to be "the heavy" at times, stand up for ourselves, set the rules and enforce them. Disciplining our kids shows that we care. It's the type of authority we choose to be that makes all the difference.

Notes:
1. Robert Shaw, *The Epidemic: The Rot of American Culture, Absentee and Permisive Parenting and the Resultant Plague of Joyless, Selfish Children* (New York: Regan Books, 2003), 34.
2. Gary Zukav, *The Seat of the Soul* (New York: Fireside Books, 1989), 199.

3. E. Timothy Burns, *From Risk to Resilience* (Dallas: Marco Polo Publishers, 1994), 24.

4. Ibid.

5. Ibid., 27. See also H. Stephen Glenn, *Raising Self-reliant Children in a Self-indulgent World* (New York: Random House, 2000).

6. Ibid., 29.

7. Ibid., 13.

8. Ibid., 13.

9. Ibid., 14.

10. Robert Shaw, *The Epidemic: The Rot of American Culture, Absentee and Permisive Parenting and the Resultant Plague of Joyless, Selfish Children* (New York: Regan Books, 2003), 117)

11. Ibid., 160.

12. Judith Guest, *Ordinary People* (New York: Penguin Books, 1976), 257.

13. Roland and Sherry C. Wong, *Chicken Parents, Chicken Schools* (Baltimore: Publish America, 2005), 17.

14. Ibid., 16.

1

This is what the kids say:
Be fair and compromise. Be flexible, reasonable, forgiving, and understanding. Be a thoughtful and calm referee, advisor, and teacher.

This is how to interpret it:
You Don't Have to Be Perfect

The above commandment is definitely asking for the ideal parent, the one we can be at least most of the time. The kids know what they want, and this is the level of calm and flexibility we aim for as parents and can be proud of in our best moments. But both you and I know that we make mistakes.

A friend told me recently that she spent two years in therapy finding out that her main problem as a parent was trying to be perfect and trying to correct all of the mistakes of the dysfunctional family she grew up in. She said she was driving herself, her husband, and her kids crazy. She thought that if she was the perfect parent, she would have perfect kids and the perfect life. Then she realized there is no such thing. One day, she gave herself permission to be an imperfect mother and had the best Mother's Day ever.

We believe in the magic equation: If we follow the expert advice and do just right thing, it will solve our problems forever. This is the magical thinking we all engage in at times, whether it's about weight loss or relationships. We want that magic bullet so badly, but life and the human psyche are more complicated than that. You will get excellent advice in this book and skills that can change your life, but the most important ingredient is you and your own integrity. We have to trust ourselves as parents, and we must be the change we seek.

Search, reflect, and persist

When my friend became conscious of what she thought she wanted (perfection) versus what her kids needed (structure, authority, and a role model), she began to give her kids what they needed. As a result, she and the kids all became more fulfilled. Both she and her kids had needed the same thing—for her to be in charge—but she hadn't realized it. What needed to happen was the parental search. My friend had to embark on a journey for the answers. What also needed to happen was for her to reflect on the journey, for, in order for her experience to make sense, she had to think about it, evaluate what wasn't working, and implement solutions.

Searching and reflection take time, time that many parents aren't willing to give these days due to hectic schedules. However, the parent who copes with her imperfection, forgives herself, reflects on her parental practice, and gets back into the parenting saddle after making a mistake will be the one who ultimately succeeds.

EMOTIONALLY STABLE AND AUTHORITATIVE

We can't be perfect, nor should we be, but we can be an emotionally stable parent so that our kids can count on us be sane and rational, at least most of the time. In a chaotic world, finding the time to assess our parental strategies can be difficult, but as Roger and Sherry Wong note, "children need parents who are emotionally stable and secure" and willing to reflect regularly on these important questions.[1] For instance, we have all fallen back on parenting practices we learned from our parents, good or bad, when we are stressed and haven't made a conscious plan of our own. We have all stepped back from being a negative disciplinarian and thought, "I can't believe I just said and did that!" These are the moments we wish to avoid.

E. Timothy Burns defines *authoritative* as a discipline style that is "warm, supportive, with clear rules and expectations," as opposed to *authoritarian*, which exacts absolute obedience without much consideration or caring.[2] The *American Heritage Dictionary* also describes the positive mode, *authoritative,* as "having or showing expert knowledge."[3] This is particularly relevant for the confident parent. As I said previously, parents can't rely solely on the experts; parents need to take back their authority and trust their best instincts. Yet I have quoted experts and said that all parents need skills. The fact is that the informed, authoritative, reflective parent *is* an expert. He takes the time to consider what the experts say, sifts through their advice and considers what works from his own experience. The expert parent embraces the role of authority because he has respect for himself and confidence that, in spite of occasional mistakes, he is worthy to guide his own children.

Parents Often Lack Self-respect

The problem with many parents today is that they lack basic self-respect. They allow their children to speak and act with disrespect toward them, and thereby send them out into the world to disrespect the population at large. This is our number one problem. In the highly-readable *Generation Me*, Jean Twenge says this lack of parental backbone comes in part from the current cultural belief that a successful person is outspoken and takes advantage of opportunity, and that this so-called "confidence" can be damaged by parental control and discipline. Generation Me includes "today's under 35 young people."[4] They are not a "selfish" generation so much as a "self-important" one, according to Twenge.[5] Where previous generations were raised to be obedient, this generation was raised to constantly question authority and put self before duty. We know where this trend came from—Baby Boomer parents who lived through the Vietnam War, the disillusionment of Watergate, Kent State, and other heartaches of the 1960s. It's all perfectly understandable.

And yet there's a difference between intelligently and thoughtfully questioning authority and allowing children to ride rough-shod over their parents, and anyone else who gets in the way. Twenge notes the positive language used to describe out-of-control children in the media these days, like "strong-willed" and having a so-called "spark that sets their tantrums into motion" and will give them, according to a certain magazine, "what they need to excel" in the competitive adult world.[6] People are willing to rationalize their children's behavior and sacrifice their own pride, apparently, so their kids can survive in the dog-eat-dog world. To me this sounds like an excuse—an excuse not to take charge, an excuse not to be "mean" so their kids don't hate them. This is, unfortunately, reflective of parents who hate themselves.

No self-respecting adult accepts disrespectful treatment. Do the parents of Generation Me really hate themselves because they now are the authority? If so, we need to get over it. I don't care what generation you're in: You only get the respect you *believe* you deserve.

I realized recently that some of our youngest students in high school (Gen Me kids) have parents who are also Gen Me. That's Gen Me kids raising Gen Me kids. That's a whole lot of self-importance and entitlement masquerading as true confidence. That's a whole lot of passive, politically correct parenting. This is not to say that young parents can't do a wonderful job. Some Gen Me parents are making genuine attempts to overturn the "me-first" reputation of their generation. Some have already shown that they are thoughtful, reflective parents, and that gives me hope.

Parenting Should Be a Joy

On my way home from the grocery store recently, I spotted a license plate frame that said, "Happiness is being the parent of 3 kids." A man was driving alone in the car, and I couldn't help wondering, *Who bought it?* I was pretty sure he didn't buy it himself, and then I realized the cynical part of me was kicking in.

Did his kids buy him the frame? Why would they do that? To make him smile on Father's Day? Remind him they exist?

Did his wife give it to him? Was this a good-natured hint from a wife who felt her husband wasn't seeing his kids enough? Or maybe she felt he wasn't "happy" enough being a father and needed reminding that he should be.

Maybe they'd recently been through a crisis with their kids and were feeling relieved and appreciative.

Or maybe, just maybe, they really do have three great kids and it genuinely makes them happy.

That is, after all, the way it should be. Robert Shaw, who, as a child psychologist, probably sees more disturbing behavior from kids than most of us, reminds us that "raising children should be a pleasure almost all the time."[7] But this pleasure, this love must be based on something. The parent-child bond must be very strong to begin with, and this bond develops in a number of ways.

The Basis for Trust

Commandment number one says we should be fair and willing to compromise. The expectation that a parent will be fair and attempt to compromise implies a history of trust between that parent and child: For the most part, the parent has acted in consistently trustworthy ways. He has earned the child's trust by being level-headed and judicious and by following through on promises in the past. This kind of parent, however, will only compromise if it is in everybody's best interest to do so. Remember the Parent Creed: *As a parent I cannot allow my child to do anything that is not in his or her best interest—or mine.*

As Bert puts it, "It doesn't matter what you do in matters of discipline that makes the difference. What makes the difference is doing what you say you are going to do." A parent who is truthful, consistent, and who follows through shows a high level of respect for himself and his child.

What Is Fair?

The word *fair* can be interpreted in many ways. One person's idea of fairness will be another's oppression. For example, you may think it fair that your newly-licensed, sixteen-year-old son is allowed to drive within a twenty mile radius from home. But when his favorite band is performing sixty miles away, and all of his friends want him to drive to the concert, he thinks your rule is unfair. What you decide in this situation will depend on your assessment of several things, including your child's maturity, driving ability, and the behavior of his friends. What you decide may very well displease him. That's okay.

You can't always be fair in your child's eyes, but you can always look and sound fair. This is a skill. According to Bert, you look and sound fair in the following ways:

- The rules of the house must be known, so that everyone has parameters. Who is in charge? (You are.) What are the house rules?
- Remember the Parent Creed: *I cannot allow you to do anything that is not in your best interest—or mine.* The prospect of your young, inexperienced driver traveling sixty miles on unfamiliar roads with rowdy friends in the car to a venue with older teens appears like an unsafe option: In your opinion, it is not in *his* best interest. You also know that, if you let him go, you'll be up worrying, and that is not in *your* best interest.
- Look Fair: Face your child and make eye contact, but don't necessarily smile. Nod and agree when you can. Show your concern. If compromise is an option (such as you driving instead), that can be discussed. Do not argue.
- Sound fair: Use the word "choice." Tell your child, "You have a

choice. If you continue to argue with me, you won't be driving the car at all. I am concerned about your safety, and my decision stands." End of conversation.

According to Bert, the parent needs to know the discussion is over at this point. The child—if there is a history of trust and consistency in the relationship—will abide by the parent's decision without a lot of fuss. He may complain (to himself) momentarily, but that is to save face, and he will settle into the caring adult's decision, like it or not. If the child acts out, the parent must be committed to standing by what he said, "If you continue to argue with me, you won't be driving the car at all." The child's privilege of driving the car is suspended until the parent decides otherwise.

No Consistency, No Integrity, No Trust

Unfortunately, many kids do not have high expectations for their parent's ability to be fair or compromising, nor do they respect him or her as a person. As an English teacher, I see such examples in my students' writing often. One of my students—let's call her Ashley—wrote of a time when she had a weekend with her divorced dad. It had been arranged that Ashley's father would take her to a Sonics game in downtown Seattle at the Key Arena. Ashley was excited because she was getting to spend time with her dad and also because she would experience the city at night, the lights, the bustle of the crowd, and the excitement of the game.

Near the arena, her dad found a place to park the car and told Ashley he would be back in a little while. She waited patiently, but a few minutes turned to hours. She knew exactly what her dad was doing because this kind of thing had happened before. They were missing the Sonics game as she anxiously checked the time on her cell phone.

Not knowing if she should call home or continue to wait, Ashley began to feel frightened, a young girl alone in a car at night on a Seattle street. Finally, she admitted to herself that her dad was not going to leave the bar to come see that she was okay. Her feelings obviously didn't matter to him, so she called the one person she knew she could rely on to pick her up, her mom. In her essay, Ashley was careful not to say anything too harsh or angry about her dad. It was very clear that she loved him; she was just sad and wished he was different. Her essay was on the value of "reliability," and Ashley had used her dad as an example of what reliable wasn't.

A child can only expect fair consideration if the precedent has been established. We send very clear messages to our children by our actions. We tell them how much we really value their feelings, their time, and their relationship with us. Ashley's father may have loved his daughter, but drinking at the bar outweighed any consideration he might have felt for her personal happiness and safety. Ashley internalized this message, and it has become part of the way she sees herself and her relationship with her father. In a conflict, Ashley would not expect her father to be "fair" or to "compromise" with consideration for her well-being because consistent, reliable caring on his part has never been established.

REALLY SEEING YOUR CHILD

Commandment #1 continues by asking us to be flexible, reasonable, forgiving, and understanding in disciplinary issues.

While adjectives like "fair" and "compromising" imply a needed foundation of trust and respect, "forgiving" and "understanding" are warmer terms, infused with empathy and fellow-feeling. "Flexible" and "reasonable" imply a willingness to bend, to see the other side, while "forgiving" and "understanding" imply an ability not just to see the other side, but to see into another human being and empathize.

Of course, there are times when parents shouldn't bend at all, and the outcome of a disciplinary measure does not have to be fair. However, when we do agree to enter into a discussion with our child about an important disciplinary or behavioral matter, we are sending a message of not only respect but acceptance and recognition. As parents we are saying, "I see you, I hear you, I recognize your feelings and viewpoint, and I accept them." That doesn't necessarily mean we will be swayed, but for a child the value of having a parent who really sees and knows him, whether he gets his way or not, cannot be overestimated.

If a child has just one parent who is capable of empathy—identifying with and understanding another's situation, feelings and motives—if just one parent is capable of seeing into the reality of the child's experience, that will be enough. For some children, on the other hand, neither of their parents are capable of empathy or they only have one parent and this parent isn't capable of empathy. There isn't a whole lot we can do about this situation except hope that a healthy adult eventually shows up in the lives of these kids.

A girl I grew up with—we'll call her Melissa—had a mother who, I now realize, was a narcissist. This woman was incapable of budging on most issues, and the entire family was expected to unquestioningly meet her expectations. What I realize now is that this mother did not have high "emotional intelligence," as we have come to describe the ability to pick up on facial expressions, voice inflection, and the feelings of others. She ruled her roost from a self-centered perspective, often misinterpreting or not really caring about the intentions of others.

By the time Melissa and I were juniors in high school, I had spent a lot of time observing her and her mother. I had never actually seen Melissa slapped by her mother, but Melissa had made many jokes over the years about her mother's knee-jerk reactions, lack of patience, and the many slaps in the face Melissa had endured for perceived disrespect. One day, Melissa came to school with her head held a little higher than normal. She smiled and said, "It's over. My mom will never slap me again." I looked at her in awe, half-expecting to hear that she'd murdered her mother and buried her in the backyard.

I leaned against the cold metal of my locker and listened while Melissa told me what had happened. About an hour before, Melissa had been leaving for school. She was picking up her keys from the dresser next to her bed. I had been in her room many times and could see the scene as she described it. She already had her coat on when her mother came into the room to tell her some plans for after school. Melissa—the typical teenager—only half listened to her mother, her mind wandering to her boyfriend and a humorous drama that unfolded the day before. She murmured a response to her mother, agreeing to whatever her mother had said, but her mother interpreted her reply as disrespectful. Melissa knew what was coming, so without thinking she reflexively caught her mother's arm in mid-air and then looked her intently in the eyes. Something rose up inside of Melissa as she calmly and steadily hissed into her mother's face, "Never, never do that again." Her mother looked stunned, as though she had been slapped herself, and backed away from the suddenly empowered girl. Melissa knew in that moment that the abuse was over. Melissa had handled her mother assertively, as one would successfully handle any bully.

Although Melissa ended a cycle of abuse that morning, she couldn't change her mother from the inside out. She couldn't ever expect her mother to be flexible, understanding, or reasonable in any situation where her mother's will was pitted against Melissa's own. There is never any room for compromise in a home run by a dictator. This is the narcissistic personality—a person focused entirely on self, someone who has a conscience and is capable of love but who is also utterly incapable of true empathy for another human being. Luckily for Melissa, her father was not a narcissist, and therefore he was able to nurture Melissa's blossoming individuality, something she so desperately needed.

Some Parents Are Not up to the Task

As we all know, there is no fairness when it comes to who gets which parents. Kids with parents who have personality disorders like narcissism, kids who have alcohol and drug-addicted parents, kids with abusive parents, and kids whose parents are perpetually absent in their lives are at quite a disadvantage compared to kids from stable families. Yet so many kids rise above their circumstances that we must acknowledge a hint of destiny here: kids learn from negative parenting, too. Would Ashley, for instance, ever dream of leaving her child alone in a car while she whooped it up in a bar? Not on your life. Would Melissa ever slap her own children? Probably not. Kids are resilient as long as they can find that one healthy adult in their time of need. We all want to be that one healthy adult and not the parent remembered for negative parenting.

Truly troubled parents are not capable of being the thoughtful and calm referee, the advisor and teacher that Commandment #1 asks of all parents. They are simply not up to the task and never will be. Some troubled parents can change but it will come late and, in some cases, too late to make any difference to the damage already done.

However, if you are reading this book, you are in the majority of parents who are capable of doing a pretty darned wonderful job of parenting. If you respect your child, respect yourself, expect your kid to respect you, embrace your authority, reflect on your practice, and are firm and consistent, you can turn around any difficult situation with your child.

HAVING A PLAN

Most of the time, we can be the thoughtful and calm referee, the advisor and teacher kids want us to be. At other times, we will lose it. However, in order to develop a more consistent practice of loving mentorship, it is necessary to have a plan. We must have some basic principles to fall back on in any situation with a child of any age. Although the following advice is framed for the parents of teenagers, it is relevant to all parents. This wisdom comes from Israeli-born child psychologist, Haim Ginott, with added insights from Simmons Associates:

- **Win them over:** You can have the most perfect logic and be right every time, but that will never win a battle with your teenager. You must, with the very essence of your character, win them over.

- **Be more human:** Ginott quoted one of his teenaged clients on her father, "I wish he were less clever and more human!"[8] *Human* means more vulnerable, empathetic, spontaneous, and appreciative of art, beauty, emotion and humor. Human beings are flawed; admit to your child that you have flaws but not in a self-deprecating way. Do not belittle or devalue yourself. You have flaws—big deal.

- **Be less concerned with being right:** You may know in your age and experience that something is true, but don't always be the first to say it. Let your teen come to a conclusion, whether you agree with it or not. Show respect for her viewpoint. It is far more important for your child to feel your love than to know you are right.

- **Don't be cynical:** Don't burst her bubble. She may live up to the ideals you couldn't.

- **Don't be hypocritical:** Your kids have heard what you "believe," and they watch everything you do. So when you say you aren't a racist but fret when the immigrant family moves across the street, they'll notice. Remember not to judge, so you won't be judged by your teenager. Be consistent; live up to their expectations.

- **Be a mature person of substance:** Teens respect people who are deep and they can spot a fake every time. They see many examples of superficiality on TV and in popular media. Balance their intake by valuing learning and real human experience versus virtual reality.

- **Deal kindly and constructively with momentary mistakes:** Teens need to learn calmness and moderation; be a model for them in your best moments. If your best moments happen far more frequently than your worst moments, give yourself a pat on the back.

- **Echo their feelings:** Make it clear you understand them and then state your wishes. "You feel we don't trust you by having a curfew. I understand that you would like the freedom of deciding when to get home. However, I worry about you when you are tired and when more drunken drivers are on the road. I trust your judgment much of the time, and I'm proud of the good head you have on your shoulders, but I don't always trust your friends' judgments. Having you home at a reasonable hour will help me sleep and keep you safer." What is good for you is good for your kids. If it doesn't work for you, it isn't going to work. Still, it's important to observe, agree, listen, and question in a neutral fashion, and then, if compromise is out of the question, hold your ground.

- **Be understanding, but not too understanding:** Ginott said, "The sad truth is that no matter how wise we are, we cannot be right for any length of time in our teenager's eyes."[9] This is exactly as it should be, for our teenagers are trying to separate and define themselves apart from us, while needing our acceptance. They will even argue when they don't really disagree just so they can bounce around an idea or an emotion, and try it on.

- **Keep the discussion brief and matter of fact:** To quote Ginott: "Teenagers do not want instant understanding. When troubled by conflicts, they feel unique. Their emotions seem new, personal, private. No one else ever felt just so. They are *insulted* when told, 'I know exactly how you feel. At your age, I too felt the same.' "[10] While it seems compassionate to commiserate, it can also be arrogant and off-the-mark to assume we know what our child is feeling. It's best to nod, listen, keep it brief, and not "make it about you."

- **Help your child by "tolerating his restlessness, respecting his loneliness, and accepting the discontent":**[11] It's so hard to accept our child's unhappiness and pain. We parents will do just about anything to make them happy again, but this can be a downfall.

Our soft-heartedness is a reason why so many of our kids are spoiled and good at manipulation: They know exactly what we will do when presented with tears and a sad face. They know their parents are a soft touch, and the old folks will ante up under the right pressure.

On the other hand, when our children are experiencing genuine restlessness, sadness, loneliness, and discontent, we must allow to them to face these difficult feelings. We can do this with respect by offering the gift of our love and understanding, and then backing off. It is their journey. They must know that we are there if they need us, but they must also know that we believe in their ability to cope.

Our Not-so-great Moments

By consistently behaving in ways that gain our children's respect, we establish a healthy base from which to conduct all issues of discipline. We win them over with wisdom and strength in our best moments, but what about our not-so-great moments?

We all mess up—yell and say things we shouldn't—leaving unresolved and uncomfortable feelings between us and our children. We are haunted by the times we didn't keep our cool, and, let's face it, some of us lose our cool far more often than can be considered healthy. For many of us, maybe the base is a little more shaky than we'd like to admit. So what can we do?

Our kids want us to be calm, level-headed parents in spite of the fact that living with kids, and especially teenagers, can be like living with lunatics. The important thing to remember is that you are the adult and that anger actually can be your friend.

THE GIFT OF ANGER

Most of us are afraid of our anger. We either feel we aren't entitled to it or we're afraid it will balloon into rage. Political correctness has invalidated our anger in several spheres but no more than in parenting, where anger is not allowed and must be replaced by endless cajoling or neglect of an issue because the parent is afraid to deal with it. In other words, parents have been stripped of their power, and a significant portion of their power comes from righteous anger.

However, before we can use anger for the benefit of our children, we have to get our heads screwed on straight about our own right to authority. If you're a Boomer parent, you grew up in a time when parental and government authority were suspect and found wanting. Now that *you're* "the man," you may like to pretend you're not.

If you're a Gen Me parent, you have been so completely influenced by political correctness that you may think it's possible to raise children without discipline, without displays of anger. Yet you blow up: you scream, you hate yourself for screaming, you may even hit them, and then you want to beat up yourself. We've all done it. You're human—admit it. It's time to make anger your friend because there's no way you can avoid it.

Claim Your Authority

First of all, you have to reclaim your authority. Take it out of the politically correct time-out where it has languished—just as today's youth languish in moral indecision. Commit to memory this statement found in *Chicken Parents, Chicken Schools,* "No one else, regardless of advanced degrees, stature, intelligence, or expertise, is better qualified than we are to make the daily decisions about our children's lives."[12]

Remember the part about you, the parent, being the single most important person in your child's life? You are the most important influence your child will ever experience, and no one else can do your job. Few of us consider the enormity of the psychological contract into which we are entering when we bring a child into the world. No one is better qualified than you to raise your child. The good news is that it actually feels good to assume your natural authority, but it's important to approach it, especially the inevitable anger you will feel, with knowledge and skills.

Anger Is Not Immoral

Even before we had politically correct parenting, many parents considered anger immoral,[13] even back in the authoritarian '50s and before. That is because anger conjures up images of rage, of irrational, scary, violent, and, therefore, damaging outbursts. Rage is built-up anger, and it *is* frightening. It can explode when we don't expect it, like a pent-up volcano, and spew forth destruction that leaves the victims and the volcano shocked and damaged.

We wonder, *Where did* that *come from?* We may be shocked by the force and the magnitude of our emotion and disturbed that it came from inside us. However, if allowed to vent at healthy intervals and harnessed for good, anger can be used as a tool in your bag of positive parenting tricks. Anger is power, and you, as the parent, must not fail to grasp it. Anger only turns into evil when it is coupled with vindictiveness, the desire to hurt.

It is perfectly all right for a child to see her parent angry. It is when a parent loses control of that anger that it becomes unacceptable.

A parent must be clear about his or her own right to be angry, and the parent must be clear about the intention behind what is said in anger. Let me give you a famous example I got from my Sunday school days. (It isn't politically correct to bring in a religious story, but then neither is it politically correct to be angry.)

Most people think that a good Christian is someone who is perpetually nice, helpful, mild-mannered, and forgiving (perhaps even to the point of being a bit of a doormat). But Jesus, who was no doormat, showed that "nice" has its limits. In the story where Jesus clears out the moneychangers in the temple, he finds the temple bustling with commerce, not prayer, and he—certainly not for the first time—is struck by the tendency in people to prize material gain over the fruits of the spirit. Immediately, Jesus flies into a rage, drives the moneychangers, along with their sheep and cattle, from the temple with a whip, scatters the coins, and overturns the tables, while shouting that they have made his house of prayer a "den of robbers'" (Matthew 21:12-13). We can assume, perhaps, that this anger had been building up for some time, but what we know for sure is how strongly he felt about the wrongness of the situation. That is abundantly clear.

Anger Shows We Care

You, as a parent, on more occasions than you wish, will be compelled to act in a way that shows that you strongly disagree with your child's behavior. These instances will usually involve your anger, and this is a good thing, for as Haim Ginott observed, "Our anger has a purpose; it shows our concern. Failure to get angry at certain moments indicates indifference, not love. Those who love cannot avoid anger."[14] Kids know this. They know that even when our attention is unpleasant, it shows we care. How emotionally devastating is it for a child to receive a parent's indifference and lack of action when a situation very clearly calls for the parent's passionate involvement?

"SOMEBODY, STOP ME!"

Kids usually don't do it consciously, but they will engineer situations that demand their parents' attention. They want to see how their parents will react, and they are hoping it will be with firmness and discipline because they need it desperately. Kids cannot be in control; they are, in fact, often out of control because they are developing beings. They wish with all of their hearts for a strong, in-control parent who can rein them in and provide care and guidance.

Jim Carrey makes it funny in the movie *The Mask* when his green-faced alter-ego flashes the toothy smile and says, "Somebody, stop me!" But I feel like our kids are saying this to us all the time. When we do stop them, with the attitude that we have the right and authority to stop them, the results are overwhelmingly positive.

As a teacher, I will never adequately come to terms with the fact that I have to discipline other people's kids. I think kids should come to school fully trained to function well in a cooperative environment—and many of them are. But all teachers have to deal with kids who are still looking for an authority figure to stop them. Having found no limits at home, they turn to the next available authority, the teacher, with an unconscious but very real hope that their search for an in-control adult will end. That means that teachers always get a few kids in each class, sometimes several, who wish to oppose the teacher or dominate and draw attention to themselves by talking out of turn or acting out in other socially inappropriate ways. Often they do this by teaming up with others or competing for attention. This, of course, detracts from the learning environment and must be stopped, which is exactly what these *Mask*-ed terrorists want.

When teaching, I'm so excited and wrapped up in the subject matter that I don't want to interrupt the lesson with heavy-handed discipline. I'll "shush" here or cast a look of derision there. I'll be patient to a point, but, if the behavior doesn't stop, sometimes I become angry. When this happens I get very intense, show my anger, tell them their behavior is absolutely unacceptable, and state the consequences if their behavior does not change.

I am not negative when this happens. I don't resort to hostility when I get angry: I don't name call, I don't raise my voice, and I acknowledge my feelings: "I am very angry and disappointed with those of you who are not focused on the lesson." It doesn't turn into a negative situation, and I am always amazed at the results of showing my anger. My admonishment brings silence, always. The class is jolted into refocusing, and the learning continues. My serious students are thankful for the action I took, and I notice that, in spite of the discomfort I feel after being the heavy, all of the members of the class become happier in the midst of restored order. They buckle down and get into the lesson, secure in the structure that discipline provides. In addition, our exchanges—at least for the next day or so—are more polite than usual, their efforts are more earnest, and some of the students go out of their way to be helpful and kind, just to please me.

At times, I feel emotional and resentful of the fact that I have to discipline other people's kids. I think: *How dare these ingrates interrupt a lesson into which I poured my heart and soul, and how dare they push me to the limits of my patience?* I have come to realize, however, that in these situations my response is to express righteous anger, and the kids know that. Their reaction is to settle down, get to work, and feel secure in the abundance of my caring. Even though it is my least favorite part of the job, I realize I am given a sacred trust when my students behave in ways that force me to be the adult. In no uncertain terms, I show them that my tolerance has limits, that I have real feelings, and that I have their best interests at heart. As a parent or teacher—a surrogate parent role—that is how we get their respect. If you're like me, you hate every minute of being the heavy, but you do it anyway because you care about your kids and what they learn.

Lack of Discipline = Lack of Empathy in Children

If children grow up without adults to stand up for their rights and feelings, they grow up with a lack of empathy. They walk into a classroom and just assume it's all about them without regard for the teacher's goals or the needs of the other students. In *The Epidemic* Robert Shaw explains, "If a child is endlessly indulged and never hears the word 'no' or experiences limits, he never has a chance to learn that other people have lives, emotions, needs, and wills of their own. Without a well-developed sense of empathy, the child will not be able to love."[15] Those are frightening words, but true ones. Kids who disrespect others, such as disrupting a class, are damaged human beings; they have been deprived of the opportunity to value and understand the rights and needs of others; they have been, to a very real degree, deprived of discipline by the people who owe them the most, their parents.

We already live in a callous culture. Movies, TV, video games, and the evening news routinely show people being used for selfish gratification. The media constantly depicts the abuse of people and the senseless slaughter of human lives. For us to enjoy the annihilation of human figures in movies and video games, we must be able to think they are expendable and not entirely like us. For their deaths to be acceptable, we cannot acknowledge that all human beings have attachments, joys, sorrows, and a need to be loved. That would make the shooting, dismemberment, and fiery explosions far less fun. So we detach emotionally; we de-sensitize.

Who stands to gain from this de-sensitivity? Certainly not the children engaged in this "playing" or TV viewing—certainly not the world at large. Courtesy, respect, and gentleness depend on the notion that people are of value and worthy of our care. To care, we must be sensitive; we must be open to the humanness of those around us. If that means rejecting popular culture, so be it. It's time for all of us to be accountable and take a stand against cruelty of any kind.

THE DIFFERENCE BETWEEN EMPATHY AND SYMPATHY

We need to nurture empathy in our children, but, as parents, ironically, our sympathy needs to have limits. Though they are often seen as synonymous, *empathy* and *sympathy* are not the same thing. *Sympathy* connotes agreement. If one has sympathy for the emotions of another, there is harmonious agreement: You're on the same page—you agree. With *empathy*, one does not have to agree with the emotion, but there is understanding.

As a disciplinarian, it is essential to respect and acknowledge feelings, but to sympathize with inappropriate behavior is to undermine your position and mission. Remember: You are standing for something. You need not agree with your child's feelings and experience. If your child has just shouted at you, you may acknowledge his strong feelings, but in no way should you sympathize with his disrespect. You can empathize, but do not sympathize. If you sympathize with your child's emotionality, if you are subject to his manipulation, your message of mutual respect will fail.

- Be understanding; acknowledge feelings, but do not engage.
- Stay focused on the issue at hand.
- Keep in mind that your adult perspective is different than your child's, as it should be.
- Expect and insist upon mutual respect.

We want our children to grow up with the ability to experience all of their feelings, but we must be a model of moderation and maturity for them. Therapist Mary Pipher said, "A society without accountability is a dangerous place. A society without empathy is fascist. A healthy society must say to its members, 'We empathize with your troubles, but you must behave properly.' A decent society teaches both empathy and account-ability. On both counts we are all in this together."[16] We want children who are sensitive to the needs of others and not de-sensitized by a brutal culture. That means that we must first be willing to show our kids that we, too, have feelings and needs and we need to show them that their actions affect us.

Using Anger Well

The use of anger in its positive form cannot be overestimated—not only for the development of appropriate behavior but for the development of empathy. Before you get mad and make it work for you, be very clear about what should and should not happen. Moments of sudden anger are the scariest for children and parents. As Haim Ginott observed, "we become temporarily insane."[17] If we don't have a set of coping skills to refer to in moments like these, we may attack and insult, we may even become physically dangerous, and then we will be filled with guilt and remorse, all of which we want to avoid. Here's what to do in cases of sudden anger:

- **Describe what you see**. Use "I" statements: "I see a pile of laundry that I asked you to do yesterday, and I see a lot homework that has not been done." or "I see grades on this progress report that are not acceptable." or "I see someone standing here who said she would be here a half hour ago."
- **Describe what you feel**. "I feel very angry and disappointed." or "I feel like you don't value your education or take me seriously." or "When you don't show up when you say you will, I get worried, and it also puts me in an uncomfortable position with others."
- **Describe what needs to be done**. "This laundry must be done today." or "Your homework must be done before you do anything else." or "It's important that you are a person of your word. That means following through on what you say you'll do."

In addition, Bert Simmons offers the Paradoxical Response. This is a skill. You train yourself to do the exact opposite of what is expected. The natural reaction to anger is for the tummy to tighten and the face to show anger and pain. Become conscious of how you look and feel. This takes control but will come with practice. Here's what you do:

- Let your tummy relax.
- Give an assured, quiet, thoughtful look.
- Let your brain take over the gut reaction. Back off, slow down.
- Lower your voice or don't talk at all.
- You may even walk away and address the issue later when you are calm.

The most important thing to remember is not to attack the character or personality of the child.

- Focus on the behavior and the consequences.
- Never resort to insults.
- Do not bring up old issues.
- Deal with the situation at hand.
- State very firmly what you need the child to do.

Once you have calmed down, you can move into being the level-headed advisor and teacher they love and adore. You can be mad, but you're under control. Kids will be convinced of the force of your conviction and depth of your love when you are intensely and righteously angry but acting responsibly and in their best interest.

Accept It

As parents, we must accept that our children will, at times, offend us, make us feel uncomfortable, hurt, irritated beyond belief, and furious. This is normal. We are entitled to all of our parental feelings without guilt or shame as long as we express ourselves positively and do not resort to insulting or abusive behavior.

Jan Faull, a specialist in child development and behavior and columnist for *The Seattle Times* put it this way, "Anger expressed on a limited basis is not all bad."[18] For example, you might say "I am very upset with you," or "I want you to know that right now I am very angry." Faull continues, "When parents express their anger with words—without using contempt, sarcasm or insults—it can sometimes change and improve children's behavior"[19] As she notes elsewhere, such conflicts can even serve to bond parent and child.[20] How many of us have not felt closer to our kids once the air is cleared and everyone is cooperating again?

The damage occurs when parents resort to disrespectful, fear-based tactics of revenge and control.

Notes:

1. Roland and Sherry C. Wong, *Chicken Parents, Chicken Schools* (Baltimore: Publish America, 2005), 57.
2. E. Timothy Burns, *From Risk to Resilience* (Dallas: Marco Polo Publishers, 1994), 104.
3. "Authoritative," *American Heritage Dictionary*, third edition (New York: Houghton Mifflin Company, 1994), 56.
4. Jean Twenge, *Generation Me* (New York: Free Press, 2006), 1.
5. Ibid., 4.
6. Ibid., 76.
7. Robert Shaw, *The Epidemic: The Rot of American Culture, Absentee and Permisive Parenting and the Resultant Plague of Joyless, Selfish Children* (New York: Regan Books, 2003), 131.
8. Haim Ginott, *Between Parent and Teenager* (New York University: The Macmillan Company, 1969), 129.
9. Ibid., 31.
10. Ibid.
11. Ibid., 30.
12. Wong and Wong, *Chicken Parents, Chicken Schools*, 52.
13. Ginott, *Between Parent and Teenager*, 94.
14. Ibid., 96.
15. Shaw, *The Epidemic*, 107.
16. Mary Pipher, *The Shelter of Each Other*, (New York: Riverhead Books, 2008), 157–58.
17. Ginott, *Between Parent and Teenager*, 97.
18. Jean Faull, "Using Anger Effectively Can Be a Challenge." *The Seattle Times*, February 24, 2007.
19. Ibid.
20. Jean Faull, "Don't Let Hang-Up Over Phone Affect Decisions." *The Seattle Times*, February 19, 2005.

2

Do not overreact and resort to irrational, ineffective behaviors like yelling and hitting or assigning arbitrary punishments that may be disproportionate to the offense.

This is how to interpret it:

Get Conscious

As parents, we have to become conscious. This means becoming aware of our behavior and motives as parents. So much of what we learned from our own parents was absorbed unconsciously, and that is why we are often so shocked (and not shocked) when we recognize their behavior in ourselves. As Roland Wong notes, "If those behaviors are things you want to continue, great. If not, then you need to consciously delve into your own childhood and identify which parenting behaviors were valuable and effective and which you want to avoid."[1]

My guess is that you will agree with your child that over-the-top rage—yelling, which usually turns to insult and criticism, and hitting, which we all want to avoid—are the worst behaviors we remember. Just as children must gain self-control, so must parents, and this requires understanding our motives before we can change.

WHY YOU OVERREACT

You Are Afraid

- We fear losing control in an argument—a volatile situation with our child—and we are afraid of losing control of our child. We think if we can't control them, we can't protect them. This is particularly true in the teenage years when they buck against our control, as they should. But really we experience fear on several more subtle and unspoken levels.

- We may be afraid our child doesn't love us. Those of us racked by guilt have this hidden fear, for not being the parent we should have been. Perhaps we were away too much, worked too much, yelled too much, drank too much, and the list is endless.
- We may be afraid our child doesn't respect us. This fear is valid if the parent has been a doormat (too permissive), absent, or abusive.
- We also overreact when we have not learned the skill of being assertive and proactive vs. nonassertive and hostile.

You Don't Have a Plan.

- We have nothing to fall back on in a crisis except the mental tapes we have from our own upbringing.
- Hostile parents do get their needs met, but it's always done at the expense of someone else. They name call, verbally abuse, physically abuse; they scream and yell. They create fear and anger. Remember, the natural thing for people to do is to be nonassertive and hostile. That is solved by education and learning something different.
- Education teaches us that we don't want to be nonassertive and hostile. We want to be assertive and proactive and have real skills.

Fight the Fear and Get a Plan

Remember that part of being an effective disciplinarian is seeing yourself as worthy of your job.

- No one is more important than you in your child's life.
- You do not have to be perfect, and it's important to forgive yourself for the times you screwed up.
- You have a right to discipline your child, and you have a right to your feelings and anger.
- Your child needs your authority and limits.

Fear is **not** a part of the authoritative parent's mission. The authoritative parent is self-confident, has a repertoire of parenting skills, and reflects regularly on the practice of parenting: *What worked? What didn't? What will I do next time?* (see Appendix B).

OTHER REASONS WHY YOU OVERREACT OR DON'T HAVE A PLAN

You Didn't Think You Needed a Plan.

If you are a Baby Boomer parent, you grew up in a time when parenting trends were changing. Parents didn't want to be dictatorial or oppressive in their parenting techniques like parents of the past. They were so idealistic that they didn't even think they needed much of a plan at all. In fact, all they thought they needed was love. "We wanted things easy. . . . We wanted to have fun. Above all, we wanted to be free to be different from the generation before us, to be free of rules, the constraints and conventions that imprisoned them."[2] This is called throwing the baby out with the bath water. Getting rid of everything, even that which is valuable, leaves you with zip to go on. So many adults who came of age in the 70s learned to fly by the seat of their pants. They were leaving the old behind and embracing the new—whatever that was.

You Believed in the Self-esteem Movement.

Remember, we're nice—too nice. At first, the self-esteem movement sounded great: building our kids' self-esteem and avoiding all that awful criticism we endured. And it was great, sort of. We need to avoid criticizing our children, but "feeling good about yourself, no matter how you act or whether you learn anything or not"[3] has not served our children, nor has it served us as their parents.

You Didn't Want to Be the Bad Guy.

You wanted to be your child's friend. Now you know kids want real parents. As Bert puts it, "You can be friendly as a parent, but not a friend." If you are a friend, you cannot disagree or discipline.

You Believed in Political Correctness.

This completely disabled and disarmed us as parents in every way.

You Became the Busiest Generation Ever.

You work more hours, play more, and stress out more than any generation before us. This leaves too little time for family and reflective thought.

You Haven't Always Trusted Your Best Instincts.
There was always an expert who knew better.

No wonder our kids think we're bipolar. We're fun, we're easy, we want to be their best friend, then we lose it. When faced with teenage behavior, without a plan, we can panic and fly into rages worthy of a psych ward.

PARENTAL RAGE

Rage Is a Result of Not Handling an Earlier Issue.

Remember that anger builds, if not addressed, and turns into something toxic. "When you lose your temper, it says that you have delayed handling an issue until your frustration and impotence have become overwhelming."[4] Show your child healthy anger as it naturally appears or you risk damaging your relationship further with negative rage talk. Bert Simmons puts it this way, "Rage results from not knowing the future: 'What am I going to do? I don't know!' The result is rage. Have a plan and skills and create the future."

Yelling and threatening inevitably turn into insults and criticism. Do not allow yourself to attack the character or personality of your child. As E. Timothy Burns warns, "when we verbally and non-verbally dictate, suggest, or imply negative expectations—i.e. calling children stupid, worthless, incompetent, etc.—we unwittingly influence their personalities and behaviors in a possibly indelible fashion."[5] Once the words are out, you cannot take them back. For every single attack on character, many, many acts of love are required to cancel it out—if it can be canceled out.

Problem: Sometimes, to avoid yelling, and conflict in general, we cop out and give in. This can be worse than yelling.

We cop out when we ignore the bad behavior and the more subtle signals our kids send us to get our attention. We do this because we are tired, lazy, hate conflict, or we're scared of our kids. The message this sends to our kids is that we are, indeed, tired, lazy, scared of our kids, hate conflict, and they aren't worth the effort it takes to step out of our comfort zone. (Forget all that self-esteem building we thought we were doing.) Many of us turn them over to the media and electronics when we "can't deal with them anymore." Sometimes we just give up and wait to see what happens, but this is not proactive, nor in our child's best interest. Lack of discipline is neglect and emotional abandonment.

The father of a teenager told me recently, "It's just easier to give in sometimes. You're tired, it's late, and you just want it to stop." With an older child, the pattern has been set. In arguments with teenagers or with little kids' tantrums, the child has been allowed to "win." The child has been allowed to behave badly and may even be placated by things. "Okay, Mommy will buy it if you'll just be good as long as we're in the store." The snowball effect of all this placating with technology and materialistic bribing is that they "whittle away at a child's character development in the long run."[6] The child learns to be manipulative and self-centered. Bribing a child teaches them to do things in a way that is illegal or immoral. The psychological contract your child has with you, his birthright, is that you are the parent and he is the child. For you to renege on your authority is tantamount to betrayal.

Solution: To avoid yelling and arguing, employ the skill of using "foggers" or being a "broken record." Teach your child how to go to the grocery store, ride in the car, visit other people's homes, play with neighbors, and so forth. Show them exactly how you want them to behave (see Skills and Scenarios in Appendix A).

Change the Negative Talk

By now, just about everybody has heard that teenaged brains are different. A teen's "pre-fontal cortex—the brain's center for moderation, impulse-control and the understanding of consequences—is still under construction."[7] In an argument with our teenager, though, we can often mirror his excesses. Our voice rises just as fast, and, before we know it, we're hurling insults. Very quickly, we find ourselves on the same not-so-honorable level of behavior. Teens have the brain excuse for their immature behavior. We don't. As parents, we must model control.

Insults can be reframed constructively. In Bert Simmons' 1993 book, *Bound for Success*, he suggests ways to change negative talk to positive talk with our kids. Examples:

Negative: "I've spent nine hours today slaving to put dinner on the table—the least you could do is help clean up!"

Positive: "Let's all do our share, and we'll have time to play a game together after dinner."[8]

Of course, everything here has to do with the parent's attitude. It's the same situation, except in the negative example, the parent chooses to feel sorry for herself, play the martyr, and lay guilt on her family—for her decision to make a dinner that apparently required nine hours of her time.

In the positive example, we detect no negativity toward the task or the family, suggesting, perhaps, that she has taken responsibility for her actions and is merely requesting help after the arduous dinner preparation. Her more positive attitude even suggests they have fun after they have finished cleaning up!

Negative: "Can't you do *anything*, right?"

Positive: "You made a mistake, but I'm proud of you for doing it yourself. It might work better next time if you . . . ."[9]

Again, it's all about the attitude. The first comment indicates a complete lack of concern for the child's feelings, while the second comment focuses on saving face, gives the child a verbal pat on the back for effort, and then offers help. The second parental voice is, indeed, the esteemed advisor and teacher my seniors admonish all parents to be. This parent has taken responsibility for his important role.

Criticism is meant to change behavior, but it mostly creates seeds of destruction in the child's mind and in the parent-child relationship. This destruction can be indelible—impossible to remove or erase. In other words, we could be saddling our children with a lifetime legacy of hateful tapes that they play over and over in their minds because the single most important person in their lives said it.

Haim Ginott put it this way: "parental criticism . . . creates anger, resentment, and a desire for revenge. There are even worse effects. When a teenager is constantly criticized he learns to condemn himself and to find fault with others. He learns to suspect people, and to expect personal doom."[10] Expressed like this, we can see why "Discipline Me Right" is the number one commandment of my seniors. The effects of negative discipline stab deep and can last a lifetime if not emotionally healed.

Notes:

1. Roland and Sherry C. Wong, *Chicken Parents, Chicken Schools* (Baltimore: Publish America, 2005), 58.
2. Wong and Wong, *Chicken Parents, Chicken Schools*, 45.

3. Jean Twenge, *Generation Me* (New York: Free Press, 2006), 57.

4. Robert Shaw, *The Epidemic: The Rot of American Culture, Absentee and Permisive Parenting and the Resultant Plague of Joyless, Selfish Children* (New York: Regan Books, 2003), 21.

5. E. Timothy Burns, *From Risk to Resilience* (Dallas: Marco Polo Publishers, 1994), 103.

6. Shaw, *The Epidemic*, 20.

7. Kathleen Megan, "The Biology Behind Teens' Temper Tantrums," *The Seattle Times*, January 30, 2005.

8. Bert and Betty Jo Simmons, *Bound for Success*, (Santa Monica, CA: Lee Canter and Associates, 1993), 49.

9. Ibid.

10. Haim Ginott, *Between Parent and Teenager* (New York University: The Macmillan Company, 1969), 77.

3

Do not abuse your child; do not misuse your power as
the adult or misuse the child, physically or verbally.

This is how to interpret it:

It's about Power

Baby Boomers have wanted to deny their power as parents, and by
extension, so have Gen Me parents. *Let's just let it happen*, they think.
But denying our power as parents is denying responsibility for the most
important job in the world.

When my seniors wrote their commandments about abuse, not one
of them implied that they were speaking of sexual abuse, and yet I think
we have to assume that the worst-case scenarios enter our minds when we
consider the "do's and don'ts" of parenting. Sexual abuse isn't something
kids are comfortable discussing, yet nearly all of them know someone
who has been sexually used, and some of them are that someone.

Over and over my seniors wrote, "Do not abuse your children." This
general and vague admonition has been placed in the discipline category
because beatings and verbal abuse are often the results of misguided
attempts to discipline. Like the rest of us, kids hear the horror stories on
the news: people who starve their children, people who beat and murder
their children, people who abandon their children. These are horrid,
extreme cases. We never hear about most instances of abuse because they
happen in private homes and often don't leave a physical mark. Yet kids
know that some parents misuse their power in a variety of ways, and
they know it is damaging and wrong. They know that "a teenager who
is repeatedly made to feel stupid accepts such evaluation as fact."[1] They
know that being physically struck feels like being hated and that any
parent who abuses his child is truly clueless and, frankly, limited.

29

NOT ALL "ABUSE" IS ABUSE

The term *abuse* has been applied with political correctness in mind to a blend of all kinds of behaviors—including both destructive abuse and potentially constructive discipline. We need to be careful about labeling all behaviors that cause discomfort and momentary pain as abuse. Roland Wong has an interesting take on this. As a teacher, he has tried everything from "the most sugary sweet sunshine positive statements to the most outrageous antics" in attempts to get through to his unruly students. While he would characterize real abuse, like the rest of us, as "verbal attacks and manipulation . . . [and] striking a child in anger . . . with the sole intent of causing physical harm," he believes that brutally honest confrontation, which can be unpleasant, produces improved behavior and a strong bond between teacher and student. Why? Because of the guts and caring it takes to be honest with a difficult kid.

However, politically correct people would say that being brutally honest is abusive because it can cause hurt and offense. As Wong puts it, "It is unsettling to have to tell a student truthfully and directly that they are disliked by many of the kids, that their behavior irritates and annoys people, that if they continue such actions their friends will be few and their future unhappy."[2] The truth can hurt, and yet it can help immeasurably. If a kid has never been told his behavior is annoying, if he hasn't been properly disciplined at home, what will his future be like?

A case in point happened in my own classroom recently. One of my senior boys had a bad case of "senioritis." It was April, and he couldn't wait until graduation. We'll call him Jason. Jason didn't see the point of school—he hated it—and regularly told us that he couldn't be bothered with college. Yet he was bright and would thoroughly engage in literary discussions. Still, Jason got into the habit of walking into class every day and declaring his displeasure with the work and with the very fact that he had to be there. On a personal note, I knew of his loving but thoroughly permissive family and wasn't surprised that Jason, spoiled and indulged from infancy, behaved in this antisocial way.

Finally, one morning I'd had enough; after all, I worked in the hated school, and these were my assignments that he perpetually railed against—and yet I liked him. I was talking with two of my senior girls before class when Jason walked in and began to bellow as usual. With a genuine smile and a chuckle, I said, "Jason, you are so rude." He was stunned. "I am not!" he insisted. "Oh, yes, you are," the girls nodded.

"What do you mean? I am not," he said, turning red.

I told him that I worked hard and whenever he made comments like that, it insulted me. "Well, I didn't mean . . . ," he mumbled and slipped away from the confrontation. The upshot was that I got a new, happier Jason every morning after that. He came in friendly and actually excited to study *Hamlet*. He almost took over class discussions because he was so into them. Something in that momentary and embarrassing confrontation released him from his habitual it's-all-about-me-and-my-ego grumping. In a way he was set free, and yet I criticized his personality, didn't I? I attacked his character—exactly what you're not supposed to do as a positive disciplinarian. But did I really attack him? No. The moment was not heated. Jason knew I liked him. I had shown caring toward him and his classmates on many occasions, and my comment was made gently. There's a difference between slandering character in anger and with the intent to hurt and telling the truth with positive intention. I wanted Jason to stop insulting my class, see what he was doing, and grow up.

When Discipline Can Be Legislated

As disciplinarians, we have to be very careful about our motives. The same words, spoken with two intentions, can come out completely differently. Kind intent can heal and teach, while the same words spoken with malice can devastate. As thoughtful, reflective disciplinarians, we must take each situation and follow our best instincts: What is best for the kid? It may not be politically correct, but it may be exactly what the kid needs.

Remember, political correctness is all about eliminating offense and abuse, which sounds fine on the surface, but it has reached absurd levels. Now discipline can even be legislated. In Europe, it is already illegal in fifteen countries for parents to hit their children for any reason. I don't condone hitting, but there's a big difference between beating a child and a pop on the butt for running out in the street.

Again, the parent is being dis-empowered. We aren't allowed to decide for ourselves what is best for us and our children in individual situations. At this writing, a bill has been introduced by California assembly-woman, Sally Lieber, that would "make any hitting of a child younger than 4 a crime."[3] The bill has been met with derision by many parents and with enthusiasm by governor Schwarzenegger, who says he didn't spank his own kids. Fine, but why are we even having this discussion? It's happening because political correctness has been so widely accepted into every facet of our lives that we hardly notice when it reaches far more deeply than it should.

We all know that the actions of truly abusive parents should stop, but how could such a law be enforced? Wouldn't it require children to turn in their own parents? After all, how else do you get into a private home? Shades of the novel *1984*, another book my seniors read, loom before us when we consider the passage of such a bill.

We must be careful to define what real abuse is and not allow some positive disciplinary practices to be lumped into a politically correct category out of a desire not to offend. The state cannot mandate what is best for families; only the parents should have that right.

Notes:

1. Haim Ginott, *Between Parent and Teenager* (New York University: The Macmillan Company, 1969), 81.
2. Roland and Sherry C. Wong, *Chicken Parents, Chicken Schools* (Baltimore: Publish America, 2005), 80.
3. Nancy Vogel, "Lawmaker Seeks Ban on Spanking Children Under 4," *The Seattle Times* (from the *Los Angeles Times*), January 20, 2007.

4

This is what the kids say:
Do not manipulate, force (coerce), assume the worst of me,
or play mean mind games in an attempt to control me.

This is how to interpret it:
Manipulation Should Never Be an Option

So far we have seen that being straightforward, clearly stating our expectations, and being honest (even brutally honest, as long as it comes with caring) is the most effective way to deal with kids. People who manipulate do so because they doubt their own power and feel they must use underhanded means in order to get what they want. This book is about regaining your parental authority and power, not doubting it, and using it with love and strength. Manipulation is disrespectful and runs counter to every positive parenting instinct.

FORCE IS THE OPPOSITE OF LOVE

Force creates resentment in kids because it implies that they cannot be trusted to do the right thing. It does, indeed, assume the worst of them. Haim Ginott told a touching story from an eighteen happen in private homes-year-old client that illustrates the opposite of force:

> While strolling on the beach, Nora . . . asked her mother: "Mom, how do you hold a husband after you have finally gotten him?"
>
> Mother thought for a moment, then bent down and took two handfuls of sand. One hand, she squeezed hard: the sand escaped through her fingers. The tighter she squeezed, the more sand disappeared.

The other hand, she kept open. The sand stayed.

Nora watched her mother in amazement and said quietly, "I see."[1]

In any kind of relationship, an open hand implies trust and the assumption that the person who is allowed to be free deserves it. Forcing your will over your child is a personal control issue unless it involves someone's safety and the rules of the household that you've set. There are times when you need to be forceful to protect health and safety, your rights as a parent, and perhaps even the rights of others, but most of the time it is wise to assume the best of your child.

EXPECT THE BEST OF YOUR CHILD

As Jean Twenge observes in *Generation Me*, "Children develop true self-esteem from behaving well and accomplishing things."[2] This starts early. Showing your child that you trust him, that he is a good person and can be relied upon, should begin in infancy. You set a pattern of trust (the attitude)—accomplishment (the result), and both you and your child will be continually rewarded by your expectations of good. If you trust someone, you are able to predict his or her behavior. If you are trusted, it is because you have behaved in predictable and consistent ways.

However, if you have not established trust with your teenager, you will need to play some catch-up. One of the best things parents can do, if they haven't done a good job, is apologize.

Apologies go both ways. At various times, parents and children alike will be on the giving and receiving end of an apology. However, it is important to keep in mind that not all apologies are made sincerely, nor are all apologies used for the sake of healing and strengthening trust. Know the difference between sincere and manipulative apologies.

Sincere apologies go hand in hand with accountability. "I apologize for what I did, and it will never happen again." Truthful intention is commitment. The apologizer means it; he is not just buying time until the next offense.

Manipulators use apologies to placate the offended person until the next opportunity to offend. For them, an apology is an excuse for inappropriateness and a vehicle to continue. They take advantage of the Christian ethic of turning the other cheek. Most people feel compelled to forgive, but don't be so quick to do so. An assertive recipient of a manipulator's apology does not automatically say, "Okay, I forgive you," but says, "I will take your apology under consideration and give you my decision later." This puts the manipulator on notice.

Expressing trust in your child does not mean you are putting on blinders. Remember that your child is a developing creature; trial and error and experimentation are part of the process. Expect the best, however, and you will be rewarded.

If you are attempting to regain trust from your child after inappropriate behavior on your part, be clear about your new intentions and take it one day at a time. Behave consistently and with integrity from this point on. Your child will appreciate your honesty and the strength it takes to change and show humility.

Notes:
1. Haim Ginott, *Between Parent and Teenager* (New York University: The Macmillan Company, 1969), 216–17.
2. Jean Twenge, *Generation Me* (New York: Free Press, 2006), 66.

5

Enforce the rules, keep me in line, hold me accountable,
and hold me responsible. Use tough love if necessary.

This is how to interpret it:
You Are the Enforcer

Notice that teens command parents to enforce the rules even before they command them to set rules. It's a matter of priority. Why have rules if they aren't enforced? These kids have seen plenty of rules set, and a lot of wimpy adults (parents and teachers) too afraid to do anything when they're broken. Teenagers are famous for breaking the rules and pushing the limits, and yet kids don't question the fact that rules must exist. They just want adults to be strong.

GOOD RULES GET RESPECT

In *Ordinary People*, Dr. Berger tries to get Conrad out of the box, to think on his own, past societal expectations and rules. In one of their therapy sessions, Conrad brings up the "million rules" there are when it comes to dating:

> Berger sighs. "Rules, again. They oughta burn every rule book that's ever been written!" [Berger says this, trying to get a rise out of Conrad, and he gets it.]
> "And where would we be?" Conrad demands.[1]

Good Question.

Then I ask my kids a similar question. But first I show them the final scene of the movie *The Matrix* where Neo is in the phone booth. He says to the dictators of his virtual world, "I'm going to show these people what

37

you don't want them to see. I'm going to show them a world without you, a world without rules and controls, without borders or boundaries, a world where anything is possible."[2] It's all quite dramatic, and the radical strains of Rage Against the Machine pump into the room as Neo hangs up the receiver, and . . . . it doesn't bring out even a shred of anarchy in my class. I turn off the video and ask them to write answers to these two questions:

1. Could we live in a society with no rules? Why or why not?
2. Are some rules more important than others? Give an example of an important rule and an example of an unimportant rule.

Not one of my students, in class discussion, has ever said that we could live without rules. It is the quality of rules that gets them talking. In fact, it's a discussion I always have to cut short due to time.

- A senior's example of an unimportant rule: not being able to chew gum in junior high.
- A senior's example of an important rule: lower speed limits in school zones because little kids can jump out suddenly in front of your car.

Rules aren't the problem. Kids know that most rules have a redeeming quality about them; in other words, rules usually work in the best interest of the people involved. They just need to understand the reason behind the rule, and they want adults, who believe in the wisdom of the rule, to enforce it.

HOLD THEM ACCOUNTABLE IN AN ENABLING AGE

While some kids have completely bought into the politically correct party line that says nothing is your fault—you're just a victim or "challenged" in some way—most kids, as evidenced by the commandment, really do want to be held accountable and held responsible by the adults in their lives.

They are learning about responsibility, but they can't totally do it by themselves yet. They don't have it down; they aren't finished products. That is why you, the adult, set the rules. However, by the lack of moral instruction I see in some of my students, I think many parents believe their kids will just absorb good values by osmosis—but from where? The TV, the Internet, their peers?

We live in a me-first culture. Generation Me, the thirty-five and under crowd, is named appropriately. When the focus is on self, there is less of a focus (or no focus) on the needs of others. However, if you are accountable and responsible, you are definitely concerned with the welfare, needs, and expectations of others. Jean Twenge describes the Gen Me attitude about self versus everyone else, "Do what makes you happy, and don't worry about what other people think."[3] She explains further, "Since we were small children, we were taught to put ourselves first. That's just the way the world works—why dwell on it? Let's go to the mall."[4]

Note that Twenge doesn't say, we *learned* to put ourselves first; she says they were *taught* to put themselves first, which implies a more active indoctrination. This indoctrination was the self-esteem movement—the cult of the individual that began in the 60s and 70s. To be fair, this movement expressed a need of the time: The individual needed more recognition after the socially rigid 1950s. But this me-first focus is now out of control, and it's time for the emphasis to swing back. We need a balance between what's good for the individual and what is good for society, but which comes first?

Bert told me about a well-known celebrity who was traveling through Heathrow airport in London and refused to take off several layers of decorative gold chains that set off the alarm at the security check point. An attendant said to the celebrity, "Come with us. You are under arrest."

"Do you know who I am?" the celebrity asked.

The attendant replied, "I'm not concerned with who you are. I'm concerned with the safety of this flight. Come with us." The good of many must come first.

Most kids want to be responsible. They know it confers on them a sense of mastery and being the good guy, which we all need. However, we are fighting a culture of blame and abdication of responsibility. Lawyers have prospered dramatically in the last 30 years through lawsuits that blame the other guy. Jean Twenge cites social critic, Charles Sykes, who wrote *A Nation of Victims*. Of our current state, Sykes observes, "the impulse to flee personal responsibility and blame others [is] deeply embedded within American culture."[5] Unfortunately this impulse to blame is passed on to our kids, even when the majority of them still want integrity in their lives.

The irony of political correctness is that it is supposed to help you feel better about yourself. If you aren't blamed or held responsible for the bad in your life, you supposedly feel better, but this goes against the best instincts for fulfillment in human psychology. Indeed, the impulse of the hero (whom we all wish to be) is to take responsibility for his actions and experience.

Bill Moyers, while interviewing the eminent mythologist, Joseph Campbell, in *The Power of Myth*, noted that the true individual—or hero—takes his wisdom from his own experience and "not from the dogma, politics, or any current concepts of social good."[6] The Hero's Journey is "mankind's one great story," according to Campbell. It is the psychological trip we all make between birth and death. Each hero must find allies, face ordeals, resist temptations, brave enemies, endure the dark night of the soul, survive a supreme ordeal, and then win the prize (whatever it may be) and take responsibility for all of it.

Politically correct dogma and its culture of blame does not exist in the realm of the hero's journey. The aim of the hero's journey is personal integrity and fulfillment, and I am happy to report that this impulse is alive and well in many of the younger generation, as evidenced in my class discussions and students' essays. My concern is that kids get little moral support from the popular culture for being a good person, and too many of them have become anti-heroes, passing the blame for their lack of fulfillment to any convenient target.

Jean Twenge predicts that things will only get worse, "Teachers will see this attitude more and more as Gen Me has their own kids and believes that they couldn't possibly do anything wrong either."[7] My hope in writing this book is that this trend toward abdication of responsibility will be reversed, and that parents and children will embrace the power and rewards of their journey through personal responsibility.

One Kid Who Has Swallowed the Party Line

One of my students—I'll call him Carl—displayed many of the current psychological ills of his generation. For now, I will focus on his penchant for blame and how it illustrates a common attitude among the young. In one of his essays, Carl described how he was grounded for bad grades right before the prom, which prevented him from celebrating with his friends and the "hot girl" who was his date.

His anger was palpable; he railed against his parents and bemoaned the terrible fate of missing out on all the fun. As I learned from his classmates, Carl was a drinker and marijuana smoker, and those activities were no doubt included in the "fun" he was referring to—that and whatever was going to happen with the "hot girl." Not for one second did Carl take responsibility for his failing grades, the reason he was grounded in the first place. As one of his teachers, I witnessed, on a daily basis, Carl's lack of focus and effort. Although he was perfectly bright, Carl chose to party and play video games into the wee hours of the morning, leaving him significantly sleep deprived. When I confronted him about being off-task, he always offered a poor-me excuse: "I'm so tired," or "I don't get this," or "I had to work last night." Nothing was ever his fault.

Carl was not a happy kid, and he was a manipulator. He tried to get me to feel sorry for him so I wouldn't insist that he perform. He didn't feel responsible for what happened to him; therefore, he was only an observer and not an active participant in his own life. In his mind, circumstances and other people were always pulling the strings.

As his teacher, I set up a plan with his school counselor and parents where we monitored Carl's behavior together. Bert Simmons uses an even more specific plan when he works with parents, teachers, and principals on student behavior issues. The adults work as a team on what they call a "Home and School Plan" (see Appendix B) for students such as Carl.

KEEP THEM HONEST

As the adults in their lives, we have to tell kids the truth about their behavior and what is expected of them in terms of their responsibility. Haim Ginott gives an example of how one of his teen clients learned exactly where he stood with his music teacher:

> "I expect you to be prepared," [the music teacher] stated.
> "But I practiced," Craig protested.
> "The written work is part of your responsibility," [the music teacher] replied firmly.
> "I see you're not a marshmallow," said Craig. "My former teacher was a real soft touch."[8]

Craig responded to a simple admonishment. Therefore, we must assume that Craig already had some experience with expectations of responsibility at home, and with his stricter teachers over the years. Craig appears to have been well socialized and normal since he only needed a firm reminder to be held accountable. With most kids, this kind of adult tone-setting, on a regular basis, will be enough to keep normal kids on track and honest. The kids will also generally appreciate it.

However, more and more teachers are seeing kids who do not respond to normal parameters. Carl, the kid who was grounded from the dance, is an example of a boy who has not been well socialized. Carl suffers from anomie—not knowing what is normal. We see this in his complete abdication of responsibility and refusal to change. In times past, assuming responsibility for one's actions was held as a given in the maturation process. We still want our kids to be responsible today, and yet we are too often willing to be soft (like a marshmallow) and make excuses.

Even successful kids can suffer from anomie. Social behavior is changing rapidly among the young, and parents and teachers can be stunned when they realize they have been left behind. I'll give you an example. At the end of each school year, I sign many of my students' yearbooks. Last June, one of my senior boys was first to hand me his yearbook. He said he wanted me to sign it before his friends did; he didn't want me to see what they would write. I thought, *Oh, boys will be boys. Ha-ha. Maybe they'll write a few off-color comments.* Well. I had no idea.

Later, I was signing the yearbook of another senior boy, an honors student who had already given his yearbook to *many* friends to be signed. On one of the pages, I was shocked to see a reference to gang rape as something they should do over the summer, and signed below it the name of one of my senior boys. Here's the kicker: Curtis, the kid who wrote it, was not a delinquent or loser kid but one of the best students in his class: attractive, well-behaved, and well-liked. I was stunned. I didn't care if it was meant in jest. In addition to that comment, I saw other lewd references written by other boys. I told the owner of the yearbook that I was upset and deeply offended. He brushed off my reaction, and I could see that he thought I was acting old and that I was completely out of touch with something considered normal by the kids. But the word got out.

Curtis heard about my disapproval and brought it up before his class started later that afternoon, "Ms. Simmons, I heard you didn't like what I wrote in Aaron's yearbook. I didn't mean anything bad by it." I told him I thought it was frankly awful, cut the conversation short, and started class. But he wouldn't let it go, and this was a good thing. It really bothered Curtis that I thought poorly of him. That day he came in after school to talk, not to apologize (that would have been admitting that what he wrote was wrong), but to try and convince me that he was still a good person. I finally told him that everything he had done over the course of the year had convinced me that he was a good kid, and that I was willing to believe that his unfortunate writing in Aaron's yearbook was a fluke. He left feeling more at ease, but I was deeply troubled.

On one hand, I was glad that he had thought about it and now understood that writing something so violent and misogynistic was offensive and unacceptable to me. On the other hand, I saw that this kind of violent and sexually explicit comment is not seen as all that strange to kids these days, even kids with good parents and stable families. Curtis didn't understand that good people do not write things like that. If you are thinking: *My kid would never write that*, don't be so sure. Writing that in anybody's yearbook back in the 1970s when I was in high school would have been strictly taboo. But yesterday's taboos are normal today.

In the 1970s, women were fighting stereotypes, insisting on respect and equality, but thirty-five years later the street language about sex and women is worse than ever. The names girls are called and the sex acts bandied about in movies and in school hallways show us that, while society has made some strides, misogyny is rampant. This is not acceptable and should not be considered normal. When the kids ask us to hold them accountable and use tough love if necessary, we must oblige. We cannot allow the ignorance or anomie we see among our young to become normal. Popular culture tells them one thing, but we must counter it with an insistence upon respect for all people.

Notes:
1. Judith Guest, *Ordinary People* (New York: Penguin Books, 1976), 138.
2. The Matrix, Warner Bros., 1999.
3. Jean Twenge, *Generation Me* (New York: Free Press, 2006), 20.
4. Ibid., 49.
5. Ibid., 150 (citing Charles Sykes who wrote *A Nation of Victims*).
6. Joseph Campbell with Bill Moyers, *The Power of Myth*, (New York: Random House, 1991), 238.
7. Twenge, *Generation Me*, 155.
8. Haim Ginott, *Between Parent and Teenager* (New York University: The Macmillan Company, 1969), 59.

6

This is what the kids say:
Do not revoke my privileges, and don't
ground me (because it doesn't work).

This is how to interpret it:
Kids Don't Always Want What's Good for Them

Apparently, some of my students have a little Carl in them. (Carl is the one who didn't get to go to the prom because of his grades.) Grounding did not "work" for Carl, but it is an effective disciplinary consequence for many parents who already have a base of trust with their kids. If a consequence doesn't work, it is because the child doesn't care about it enough or the parent is not enforcing the consequence. In these cases, another consequence needs to be chosen that the kid really cares about and it needs to be enforced.

For many parents and their kids, grounding works just fine. Grounding is the revoking of a significant privilege, the freedom to leave the house. If you can follow through on the role of jailer, great, but most parents aren't home enough to enforce grounding, and some are too chicken to stand up to their child's pleas for release. There's also that problem of sneaking out—through a window or while the parents are asleep; my seniors write about this in their essays all the time. Like Carl's parents, you may need stronger measures, or maybe just a different, more realistic, consequence.

Revoking privileges is probably the best leverage parents have in many situations. Prioritizing a child's privileges in the order they will be taken away is a useful visual for both you and your child. For example:

1. Cell phone use
2. Having friends over
3. TV or Internet use
4. Going over to friend's house

This is called the Home Plan. (For the complete School and Home Plan, see Appendix B) First offense: the cell phone gets taken away. Second offense: no friends over (and you still have no cell phone). Third offense: no TV or Internet (plus no friends and no cell phone). Fourth offense: no socializing at all. Rarely will it get to this point. You have taken away everything a teenager lives for. For younger kids, the list will be different and reflect what they live for.

Again, if you have a base of respect and trust with your child, there's a greater chance your kid will cooperate with the punishment you offer. But with kids like Carl, kids who are not well bonded to their parents and suffer from intense anomie, you will get an attitude of "poor me" and plenty of non-cooperation. In tough cases, you will need to get tough. It will be hard, for instance, to enforce "no Internet use," when your child has a computer in his room. In that case, you will need to take the computer out of his room. Always choose a consequence that will really stick and that you will be able to enforce.

As Roland Wong points out, "Decades of research have repeatedly shown that children thrive in environments where three conditions exist: guidelines, monitoring, and consequences."[1]

- Clearly state your expectations for behavior.
- Observe your child's behavior; be there to watch.
- Have the consequences ready and be ready to enforce them. This requires thinking in advance and having a plan.

Remember that a privilege is not a right—it is earned. Remind your child of this fact. State that you are confident she can live up to your expectations and that things will return to normal when she has earned the privilege back.

So, pretty much, I'm saying to ignore what the kids said about grounding and revoking of privileges. After all, their perspective is more than a little biased.

Notes:

1. Roland and Sherry C. Wong, *Chicken Parents, Chicken Schools* (Baltimore: Publish America, 2005), 243.

7

This is what the kids say:
Set rules, limits, and boundaries, but make them reasonable

This is how to interpret it:
Teach the Rules

My seniors commanded enforcement of rules more often than they commanded the setting of rules, which shows their need for being held accountable, but, obviously, the rules must come first. One thing the kids wrote again and again was that the rules should be reasonable. "Have a real reason," they said. As long as you, the parent, set rules that ensure the well-being of both you and your child, you will always have a real reason. For example, a bedtime rule ensures that your child will get enough sleep to be healthy and focused in school:

- 6-year-olds need 10 to 12 hours
- 7- to 12-year-olds need 10 to 11 hours
- 12- to 18-year-olds need 8¼ to 9½ hours

You can explain to your child that growing bodies need more sleep than adult bodies and that dreaming is necessary for healthy psychological functioning. A bedtime rule also benefits you, the parent, by eliminating bedtime arguments and giving you some adult time before you're ready to go to bed. Once you have your reasons, be willing to enforce the rule.

IT'S YOUR RIGHT

Setting the rules is your right as a parent. Remember, the family is not a democracy. Setting expectations and guidelines for behavior "implies that you are the adult and that you have special knowledge and maturity that children don't have."[1] Children are developing creatures, but they can be well-behaved.

You have a right to a peaceful home and well-behaved children. It is when parents lose sight of their rights and authority, when they lack necessary parenting skills, that they allow their children to rule the house. We've all seen how unpleasant, chaotic, and full of conflict a home run by children is.

These kind of parents are afraid of damaging or stifling their children, they're afraid their children will hate them, and they're afraid that they as parents will be judged by other adults if they get tough. Entertaining and placating children who have been allowed to become little dictators can be exhausting. As child psychologist, Robert Shaw, points out, "family life for many has become too much work and too little fun"[2] Instead of enjoying each other's company, "we find ourselves slaving after children who laugh in the face of our weak attempts at discipline, demand to be amused all day, and stay up late because we're too exhausted to put up the struggle it takes to get them to bed. These kids are fully in charge."[3] Remember the Parent Creed: *I cannot allow you to do anything that is not in your best interest—or mine.* Some things are non-negotiable.

Resentment Results from a Spoiled Contract

Unrestricted bad behavior builds resentment in parents. They feel betrayed by their offspring, upon whom they have lavished affection and material things. However, most parents do not acknowledge or admit to the resentment. Instead, it comes out in snide comments or rage. These outbursts are not always directed at the kids—sometimes they are aimed at their partner. The kids feel resentment toward their parents, too, because the parent-child contract has been violated. Parents are supposed to be in charge and take action when a child misbehaves. Everyone knows this, and a parent's lack of action can feel like a lack of caring, a lack of love. As a result, we have a generation of kids with serious bonding issues and the highest rate of teenage depression ever.

A researcher at Ohio State University recently found that young adults who had behavior problems as children—temper tantrums, bullying, destructiveness—were more prone to emotional trouble. "Compared to their better-adjusted peers, children with a history of behavior disorders, once they entered adulthood, achieved significantly lower levels of overall happiness, life satisfaction, and self-esteem. They also report weaker rapport with relatives, poorer relations with their parents, and in general more difficulty establishing intimacy."[4]

I know of a girl who ran wild as a toddler. At two years of age and standing about 2'8," she terrorized her kind and politically correct parents with screaming, tears, and whining on a daily basis. She eventually grew out of the anti-social behavior but experienced depression as a young adult and had difficulty bonding with others, in spite of academic success and supportive parents. Terribly worried, her mother fretted when her daughter showed no interest in serious relationships and was depressed and unmotivated, even after an expensive private school education.

The wound in childhood, when parents do not step up to their role, remains with a child and can come out as bitterness (resentment), passive-aggressive behavior (punishing the parents), and depression ("I wasn't worth disciplining"). Therefore, it is extremely important that toddlers be given limits and expectations, just like older kids. Here's what you do:

- Tell your toddler "no."
- Instead of hitting, get down to the toddler's eye level. This can be very effective. Look her level in the eye.
- Speak to her in a serious tone and let him know exactly what you expect and what the consequences will be if he doesn't behave. Have a plan.
- Follow through.

Toddlers need the structure of routines—including discipline routines—to feel safe, valued, and secure.

YOU ARE THE MANAGER

It's your house, and you're the loving adult in charge. All children want limits. This means "limits on when they go to bed, when they do their homework, when they watch TV, what they eat, who they play with. And they thrive in tightly managed environments."[5] Rules are usually spoken, but it doesn't hurt to write them down and post them on the refrigerator once your child is old enough to read. For instance, your eight-year-old may need some reminding:

Ryan
1. Put your bats and balls away after practice.

2. Have homework done by 7:30, so you can watch some TV.

3. The ratio of reading to video game play must be equal.

4. Use an indoor voice with your little sister.

5. No running in the house, even when your friends are over.

I post some basic class rules for my seventeen- and eighteen-year-olds at school, which makes my expectations more immediate and real. For instance:

1. Follow directions.
2. No electronics of any kind are allowed during class.
3. All electronics must be put away and out of sight by the time the bell rings or you will receive detention.
4. I do not accept late work.

Of course, when kids are older, some house rules can be negotiated if they have earned it. Teens constantly seek more autonomy—to be more self-governing. To show your trust in them, you can give them more freedom, but it's completely up to you. If firm limits have been established early on, the raising of your child will not be the exhausting circus of so many households but the true joy it is meant to be.

Notes:
1. Roland and Sherry C. Wong, *Chicken Parents, Chicken Schools* (Baltimore: Publish America, 2005), 244.
2. Robert Shaw, *The Epidemic: The Rot of American Culture, Absentee and Permisive Parenting and the Resultant Plague of Joyless, Selfish Children* (New York: Regan Books, 2003), 16.
3. Ibid., 17.
4. Knoester as quoted in Shaw, *The Epidemic*, 128.
5. Shaw, *The Epidemic*, 129.

8

Respect me, and do not allow disrespect toward
yourself. Show that you trust me. Never give up
on me. Reward and praise good behavior.

This is how you interpret it:
Respect Goes Both Ways

We've talked about the supreme importance of respect, parents
respecting their own authority and not allowing disrespect toward themselves. We've also talked about respecting the developmental needs of
your child for discipline and authority and how you must never walk
away from that responsibility.

More than anything our kids need our belief in them—that they
are good people, loving people, strong and capable people who can pull
through any negative behavior and mature accordingly. "Never give up on
me," they say. We are in it for the long haul, and they want us there, even
if they don't always act like it.

PRAISE THEM—BUT BE CAREFUL HOW YOU SAY IT

Praising the good efforts of a little person is pretty straightforward.
Statements like, "You are such a wonderful helper!" and "What a good
writer you are!" go down well with the under-twelve crowd. But teenagers are more sophisticated and less secure in some ways about their
developing individuality. Therefore, praising them can sound like evaluation, which in turn sounds like judgment. Even if it's positive evaluation,

they don't necessarily trust it or feel comfortable with it. When praising teenagers, it's best to address the effort or the accomplishment and your feelings about it, rather than focusing on the teen's character: "I love this essay!" or "Your car looks great with the detailing." or "This project look a lot of hard work, and I'm proud of you."

At the same time, in more quiet moments, it can be meaningful to compliment your teenager—as long as the compliment is sincere and deserved—but use the "I" statement. Statements such as, "I really appreciate your honesty," and "I admire the way you've stuck to this task; it has definitely come out well," are better than, "You are such an honest person!" and "You're so committed to excellence!"

The last two compliments are evaluations and imply pressure to perform that way every time. Teens don't appreciate this, but they love your recognition. If you feel that speaking to your teen is sometimes like walking on eggshells, you're right. Just remember to stick to the "I" statement and avoid evaluation. Describe what they've done, and say that you're proud of them. "You've taken the colors in this painting and used in them in such a complementary, pleasing way!" "That outfit looks great on you!" "This progress report makes me feel very proud of you."

Reward, but Don't Overdo It

Too often these days, kids expect to be rewarded for breathing. Intrinsic rewards, what we feel on the inside after accomplishing a feat of value, feelings of competence, worth, and mastery, are often overshadowed by the desire for material rewards and instant gratification. The culture certainly has and perhaps even we ourselves have trained our kids to be superficial in this way. Remember that the self-esteem movement has told them they are special, and it is supposedly the adult's job to constantly provide that confirmation. Roland Wong offers an example of this kind of nickel-and-dime-us-to-death entitlement many kids feel. He writes, in *Chicken Parents, Chicken Schools:*

> I have a number of students each quarter who have trouble getting to class on time. After two or three tardies, they experience the consequence set out by our attendance policy—detention. Often, when they arrive on time the next day, they will ask me what they get for coming to class on time that day. Needless to say, I quickly disabuse them of the perception that making it to class on time one day is a significant achievement that deserves reward.

Used to bribes, many kids will actually request them. "If I make it to class on time, will you give me something?" Their requests range from a piece of candy to a smile or a pat on the back. To these requests I respond:

- No. Being on time shows respect for one's teacher and classmates, for their time, and for the learning environment. Being late is a disruption of the educational process.
- No. Basic respectful behavior is its own reward.

Unfortunately, too many kids don't get the respect they owe others. Another problem for teachers is that too many kids don't value education because it isn't valued at home.

For Gen Me kids, it is all about them and not the needs of others, so it is our duty, as the adults in their lives, to "disabuse" them of this me-first fallacy. They are developing creatures and can change with our help.

KIDS WANT TO BE GOOD

By age seven, with consistent love and discipline, most kids are natural humanitarians.[2] Their moral sense is developed enough that they want to do the right thing for its own sake. This is when parenting gets really good. You have this adorable child with a conscience and compassion for others, who wants to help out and please you and still thinks you're the greatest person in the world.

Now, when they're teens, they've seen your imperfections, but they still wish to please you all the same. One of my senior girls, whose mother was fighting cancer, said, "Unlike a lot of kids you see at high school, where you hear swearing and see kids doing stuff behind their parent's back, I would never think about doing such things because I know that it would hurt my mom badly."

This quote displays the kind of loyalty that a disciplined, well-bonded child has with her mother. This student also expresses the empathy that develops only in a secure, loving parent-child relationship.

Never Give up on Them

In addition to mutual respect and trust, kids also say that it important for parents never to give up on their kids. Unfortunately, when he works in schools, Bert often sees parents who have given up on their kids. They throw up their hands, they cry, they say they don't care anymore—but they do. They just haven't decided yet to assume their rightful role. They haven't yet taken charge. Here's how Bert Simmons coaches parents who have given up. In his own words:

> I was invited into an office where a vice principal was talking to a mother and father about their eighth-grade daughter, who was sitting right there in the conference. The girl had been truant from school for eight days, and the vice principal was saying, "We need to be working to get her here," when the mother broke in with, "I don't care anymore."
>
> We all looked at the mother as she continued. "She's split my family apart. My husband wants to leave me. She's not sensitive to anything. And I just don't care anymore!"
>
> That's when I asked to have the girl leave, and then I looked over at the mother and I said, "You said you didn't care anymore. Are you telling me that you don't care about your daughter?"
>
> And then she said just the opposite and burst into tears, "I love her so much. I just don't know what to do." Saying she didn't care was a lie; it was a manipulation.
>
> I hear a lot of "I don't cares." Both parents and kids use it. It is a manipulation designed to get people to plead with you, and it is designed to hurt. There's also "you don't love me" "you don't like me" and "I don't like you." These are all manipulations.
>
> Crying can be a manipulation. Crying gets sympathy. It's okay to empathize because it means "I can see how you feel, but I don't necessarily agree." Sympathy is agreement with the feeling. Do not sympathize with a manipulator. Your aim is the truth. Giving in once in a while is fine, but if you're giving in all the time, if you have no backbone, if you don't stand for anything, that's when you lose respect.
>
> If you're going to be assertive and a leader, you have to be able to spot manipulation.
>
> The tricky part for each of us as a parent is being able to spot manipulation in others but also being able to spot it in ourselves. In this family, both the daughter and the mother were manipulators. They used crying and hurtful words like, "I don't care," and "I hate you," to manipulate situations. These were lies and got them nowhere. This mother needed to be coached to assume her adult role and break out of the childish posture of a manipulator. She was encouraged to approach her daughter from a loving, authoritative stance and replace the negative talk with assertive, caring instruction.

This mother was told to write up a Home and School Plan (see Appendix B), and she was instructed to say to her daughter, "Rebecca, your father and I expect you to be in school every day. Here is how it will go: Dad will bring you to school in the morning and will walk you into Principal Sullivan's office. Mr. Sullivan will walk you to your first class, and from there all three of us expect you to be in every single one of your classes during the school day. You will go to each class, and you will get there on time.

"If for any reason you are marked absent in a class, you will have a privilege taken away for the first offense, as we discussed in the Home and School Plan. First it will be your cell phone. Then if the misbehavior continues, it will be the car, then the computer, and on down the list, as we discussed. Once you are back on track, all of your privileges will be returned to you. I will be in daily communication with Mr. Sullivan about your attendance. Do you understand?"

The Home and School Plan ensures that the child is fully aware of the expectations of the parents and educators. In fact, the child is instructed what to do, each step of the day. The parents need to remind him often of the desired behaviors in a calm, matter-of-fact tone. Through cooperation between the parents and the school official, the child sees caring and authority on more than one level: In fact, the child sees that no one is giving up on him. He has incentive to behave well (he gets his privileges and your approval), and, with follow through on the adults' parts, he feels secure that someone more mature than he is in charge. Remember: kids want to be good, and they want their parents to say what they mean, and mean what they say.

Notes:
1. Roland and Sherry C. Wong, *Chicken Parents, Chicken Schools* (Baltimore: Publish America, 2005), 248.
2. Robert Shaw, *The Epidemic: The Rot of American Culture, Absentee and Permisive Parenting and the Resultant Plague of Joyless, Selfish Children* (New York: Regan Books, 2003), 160.

9

Let me handle my own issues, including my own mistakes. Do not "pester," "nag," "lecture," and "hassle" your teen about things she needs to do or did wrong.

This is how to interpret it:
Don't Hover

This is the commandment aimed at helicopter parents who hover, meddle, interfere, and take over due to their own perfectionism and fear of losing control. Yes, teens often need reminding. As a teacher, I remind my students of what is due, but I also expect them to write it down. My care-taking has limits. Teens *want* responsibility and independence. They *want* to learn on their own, mistakes and all! We have to give them this gift. If we don't, they will resent it, and they will not learn the consequences of their actions. We can do this without saying, "I told you so" or criticizing, if we remember it is their birthright to make mistakes.

Making mistakes is how we learn. If your parents had protected you from your first boyfriends, how would you know the difference between a good man and the type you should stay away from? If your parents had driven the car for you when you got your permit, how would you have learned to be a good driver? Some things—many things—we must learn on our own. But too many young people aren't learning the consequences of their actions "because parents are routinely rescuing them from experiencing the natural consequences of their behavior."[1] Remember, as parents we're nice—too nice. It takes guts to watch your kid learn the hard way. Muster your courage and know when to back off.

BEWARE OF MANIPULATION

At the same time, we have to be aware of when our kids are manipulating us with language. If you are a strong parent and you see that your kid needs reminding (he can call it nagging if he wants), you're going to do what is in his best interest: you're going to remind or nag him.

On the other hand, some parents certainly go overboard in the "lecturing" department. They not only repeat themselves endlessly and harp away on their kid's deficiencies, but it seems they just enjoy hearing themselves talk. As Bert puts it, "Negative parents don't have balance." Parents with balance don't lecture on and on. It's important to keep in mind that you're winning them over, which I wrote about earlier. You win them over by keeping the disciplinary discussion brief. (When you're enjoying each other's company, you can talk all you want.) You win them over by not being concerned about being right all the time. You aren't going to bore them, and you'll only "hassle" them if they need it. Parents with balance do not need to hammer away at a point.

Verbal manipulation by kids and the use of negative words serves to disorient you from your purpose of discipline. Words like "nag" and "hassle" are designed to make you feel guilty—and, well, geeky—so you will back down. "Only uncool, geeky parents nag and hassle," they'll say. Don't buy into it. Let the words slide right off you. Stay focused on the issue at hand and keep it brief.

Practice Makes . . . Not Perfect, but Good Enough

Now that the revolution of the individual, begun in the 60s and 70s, has come full circle in our culture, we are able to see how it has helped and how it has hurt us. We now know that to be an effective disciplinarian, we do not have to be dictatorial and oppressive.

We now know that our children's developmental needs require us to be firm, loving, and consistent. But we may still be brainwashed enough to think that anger is wrong and discipline is mean. One of my favorite movie lines is from the 1983 movie *The Big Chill* when Glenn Close tells her daughter "no" over the phone. In the most reasonable, calm voice imaginable, Close tells her movie daughter that when she is a mommy she can be mean, too.

If you doubt your ability to change your parental behavior and be as assertive as your child needs, remember that you can fake it for a while. Yes, fake it. That doesn't mean your intentions are fake—your kid will sniff that out in a minute. It just means that you may need to act first before you can really feel the part.

I went with a friend to her church one Sunday and her pastor described how this works. He was talking about loving your neighbor, but it applies to any wish for change. "Folks," he said, "I realize you may not, right now, love your neighbor—your 'neighbor' being anyone you find difficult to love. But you can love them eventually if you act like you do. Act as though you love this person when you see her. Smile when you see her. Ask her how she is. Tell yourself you care about her answer. Listen, really listen. Nod your head as a concerned, attentive person would. Go through all the motions. Do this every time you see her. Act as though you love her, and, eventually, you will." We are capable of changing from the outside in.

Parents looking to change can do the same thing. You know what an assertive, caring disciplinarian acts like. Go through the motions, whether you feel it yet or not. Set the rules. Stand by the rules. Enforce them. Respect yourself and your child. Do it every time. You may mess up. You don't have to be perfect. Just act strong and authoritative and, eventually, you will be.

Notes:
1. Roland and Sherry C. Wong, *Chicken Parents, Chicken Schools* (Baltimore: Publish America, 2005), 249.

Appendix A:
Skills and Scenarios

These real situations, explained by Bert Simmons from his experience as a father and as a consultant in secondary schools, will provide specific coping strategies that will assist you in acting on your parental authority and communicating your concern and love to your child. While most of these scenarios will address the interactions of parents and teenagers, some may be used with younger children appropriately at your discretion. A guide to all action plans and skills may be found in Appendix B.

SKILL: IDENTIFYING THE ANATOMY OF AN ARGUMENT

Arguments never start with the child. An argument starts the second time the adult opens her mouth. So if a parent says to a child, "Please clean up the table after we eat." And the child looks at the parent and says, "I don't want to." The argument hasn't started yet.

When the adult makes the second statement, that's when an argument can occur. If the adult says, "Don't argue with me about this," the argument has started. Then the child will say something like, "I just don't want to do it." And the parent will say, "Well, you'd *better* want to do it." The argument escalates:

"Well, I don't want to. Quit yelling at me!"

"I'll yell at you whenever I want to."

"You always yell at me." See how it's a bouncing argument, back and forth, back and forth? That is determined by the adult. The adult needs to understand how a "fogger" and a "broken record" work, and that the child usually needs to be given a choice.

Fogger—Broken Record—"You have a choice."

A fogger sounds like this: "I understand," "I see," or "Uh-huh." Silence is a fourth option.

The child says she does not want to clean up the table when asked to, or she says she has something else she has to do. Looking at her directly in the eye, you say, "I see." If she turns and moves away, you call her back and become a broken record: You ask her to clear the table again. If she doesn't turn away but keeps saying she doesn't want to or she has something else to do, just keep looking her in the eye, and repeating, "I see."

Foggers are followed up with a broken record, as in the following conversation:

"Please clean up the table after we eat."

"Well, you're always picking on me."

Broken record: "You need to clean up the table."

"Well, you never say anything to Jody; she can do whatever she wants."

Fogger and Broken record: "I understand. You need to clean the table when you're finished."

That is the way you break the anatomy of an argument. You don't engage. You don't go where the child is trying to lead. You don't confront, you don't name call, and you don't let yourself go to that level.

Normally you will only need to do the fogger and broken record about three times because most kids can't stand the repetition, and they'll just disengage and obey. But some kids can take anything, so they will continue to argue with you even though you're fogging and being the broken record. You're doing what you should do, but the child won't respond.

So, after you get to your third fogger or broken record, then you say, "You have a choice." (This is when you come to the leadership role of being a parent.) You say, "You have a choice: If you continue to argue with me, you will go to bed an hour early tonight" (or you will not drive the car or whatever punishment you decide is appropriate). And then it's over. As the parent, you need to realize it's over at this point. You can even walk away.

Scenario 1—The Oppositional Child

Your oppositional child is still arguing even after you have used foggers, been a broken record, and told him he has a choice. Now you need to be proactive—you need to think ahead. Walk away from the argument and get a plan. You can come back to the discussion when both of you have cooled down.

You can plan ahead by saying to yourself, "What would I do, if my child did the following thing . . . like leaving the house with the car keys against my will, or what if he came home drunk, or what if he stole money from me . . . What would I do?" You need to think about that in advance, before you even get into an argument with your oppositional child. You need to have a plan in place. This plan will need to reflect what you can realistically do. If grounding is not practical, then you need to limit his use of the car, or you need to take away his cell phone, or cut off the allowance, whatever you can realistically do—do it. Then stand by it. As calmly as possible, assure the child of your caring and love. Remind him, "Who is your father?" or "Who is your mother?" Re-establish the hierarchy in the relationship.

When a child totally violates the respect issue and goes against your wishes, you need to re-establish respect with that youngster, and that is often done with tough love. Parents who have been negligent will most often have to play catch-up where respect is concerned. However, if you have established an attentive, respectful relationship—a true bond—you usually will not need to resort to emergency disciplinary measures. It's like the difference between putting on a band-aid and triage. Most kids will respond to foggers and the broken record.

Scenario 2—Discipline a Day at a Time

Parents need to be careful about setting time limits like, "Okay, you're grounded for six months." Don't go there. You should discipline a day at a time. Instead say, "The car will be off limits to you a day at a time until I see a change in your behavior." The quick fix is the automatic grounding, but it doesn't work because it isn't a realistic consequence, and most parents are inconsistent—they cannot follow up on what they say. Consistency is the name of the game.

It doesn't matter what parents do. What matters is if they do what they say they're going to do. If they follow through—that makes the difference. If you talk to parents who have raised good kids, it's not what they've done; it's whether they followed through on what they said they were going to do.

Scenario 3—How Far Can They Drive?

A kid gets her driver's license and wants to drive fifty miles up the road to go to a football game on a Friday night. Her dad says, "No, you can't go." Five thousand American kids die in car accidents every year. This dad has a right to be concerned.

"But, Dad, my friends are going to be with me, and it'll be fun."

The parent says, "Look, it's raining in southern California. When that happens on the freeways, they become ice rinks. I know you're a good driver, but it's Friday night. There will be drunks out on the highway, and I'm not going to pick you up in a body bag on Saturday morning. No, you can't go."

The point in this type of discipline is found in the Parent Creed: *As your parent I cannot allow you to do anything that is not in your best interest—or mine.* This scenario illustrates the "or mine" aspect of the creed; as the parent, this dad is not comfortable with this situation.

Scenario 4—Delaying the Confrontation

My neighbor told me about a Saturday morning, when his youngest daughter (whom we'll call Cassie) was eight. My neighbor was cooking breakfast that morning, making eggs and bacon.

Cassie walked into the kitchen, and she said, "Geez, it stinks in here!"

My friend didn't say anything, but it really hurt him. It was like somebody had just driven a nail through his heart. He thought, "Wow, I'm going through all this, and this is her response?" It didn't stink either—it was the good breakfast smell of bacon and eggs, toast and coffee.

But he didn't say anything in response. He thought, "How am I going to do this?" Then he referred back to the premise that said, "Don't talk to your kid when you're angry. Wait until you're calm." Now was a perfect time to implement this strategy because he was hurt, but he was also angry. He thought, "Who does this little kid think she is?"

The family was going to the beach in San Diego for the day, so as they were in the garage loading up, my friend pulled Cassie aside and said, "Cassie, when we get back from San Diego, I want to talk to you about something."

Cassie got in the car and said to her mother, "What does Dad want to talk to me about? Dad, what do you want to talk to me about?"

"I'll talk to you about it when we come back," he said. He wanted her to think about it. They drove to San Diego and came home about four hours later—which was like a lifetime for the daughter!

They came into the house, brought all of the stuff back in, and the father was ready to confront Cassie. He walked in the living room, sat down and said, "Cassie, come in here." It was now four hours after the event; my friend's emotions were way down and he was now very rational.

Cassie came in and said, "Yes, Dad, what is it?"

Then he explained to her, "You know this morning when you walked in the kitchen and you said, 'It stinks in here'? I want you to know that really hurt. And I want you to know something else: I don't want it to happen again. I want that to never happen again. You weren't thinking. You weren't thinking of my feelings, and if you do that with others, it won't be good, so don't let it happen again."

It can be effective to postpone your response to an upsetting situation. It puts you squarely in charge of the confrontation, it makes the kid think, and the extra time helps you decide exactly what you want to say.

SKILL: IDENTIFYING MANIPULATION

People, including kids, engage in a variety of manipulative behaviors, which are attempts to influence others for personal gain. This often involves devious methods designed to misrepresent the truth. As a parent, your aim is to guide your child toward truth and love. Manipulations cannot be tolerated. Children use the following behaviors to manipulate:

- Blaming
- Apologizing
- Confronting
- Making excuses
- Being overly emotional
- Being silent
- Saying "I don't care"

There are false apologies and real ones. A real apology can be healthy; a false apology is a manipulation. Similarly, an overemotional child can indicate true distress, or he could be using it as a manipulation. Being able to tell the difference is a skill.

When manipulations occur:

- Use foggers:
    "I understand," "I see," "Uh-huh." Listen and don't be defensive.
- Use key phrases:
    "Have I described for you the seriousness of this situation?" Then describe it. "I see you're upset (or frustrated), but you must do your homework" (or you must do your chores, or

you must speak to me in a respectful manner, or whatever it is).

- Refocus the conversation (bring it back to the topic at hand) with key phrases:

    "Let's remember what happened. You took the car when you weren't supposed to," or "You hit your sister, and that is never to happen again," or "You used foul language, and that is never to happen again."

    "I want you to remember that I cannot allow you to do anything that is not in your best interest or mine."

- Stay firm but fair. Remember to look and sound fair. Offer a choice.
- Express concern for your child's welfare. Express love in a calm, unemotional way.
- Ask for more information.
- Help to problem solve.

Scenario 5—The False Apology

A lot of people, including kids, apologize insincerely for saying something inappropriate or hurtful in anger, "Oh, I'm so sorry, Mom, that I came into your office and yelled at you. It was awful. I'm so sorry. Will you accept my apology?"

Many people will just say, "Sure, okay."

But I don't say that anymore. I say, "I'll take it under advisement." People establish a method of operation, and they will do it over and over. That's the way they get rid of their anger: they become hostile, take it out on somebody, stomp out, and then a day later, they'll beg forgiveness: "Mom, I'll never do it again," or "Mom, I'm really sorry."

It's okay to forgive, but the person forgiving needs to use it as a teaching tool for the other person. Don't be so quick to accept the apology. Instead say, "I'll take it under advisement, and I'll let you know how I feel about it later."

If a parent automatically accepts an apology from a kid, it is confusing to the kid. He wonders, "Does this mean that what I did was okay? I can blow up and then ask forgiveness and be forgiven? Cool!" It invalidates your anger and what happened.

The bottom line comes when the parent insists to the child that it will never happen again. The kid must be sincere this time in the apology. "I'm sorry. I shouldn't have done it, and it will never happen again." Now we have a commitment.

Scenario 6—"I Hate You, Mommy!"

A young mother told me about her six-year-old son who shouted at her and called her names when she had to go to work in the summer time. For the most part a happy, well-behaved child, this boy would lash out when he perceived that his major source of entertainment (his mother) was leaving him, and he would have to go to daycare. The mother told me that her tactic was to ignore him, listen to the crying and the hurtful words ("I hate you, Mommy!" plus a few expletives) and wait for an apology. Finally, after the little one had sulked away to his room, he would return and tearfully offer an apology. The mother thought her tactic of ignoring the child worked because she eventually got an apology, but the fact is that she willfully allowed her child to disrespect her. She allowed him to say terrible things to the mother he loved. She allowed herself to be abused, and she allowed her son to be an abuser! This entire scenario can be avoided, I told her. Then I told her what she needed to do:

The next time your son becomes upset and attempts to manipulate you into staying home with him (because that is what he is doing, or at the very least he is punishing you for leaving), you need to get down on his level and look him in the eye. If necessary, use foggers until he calms down enough to listen: "Uh-huh, I understand, I see," and so forth. Then, when he's ready to listen, say in a calm, firm voice, "I can see that you're upset, Coltan, but you must never speak to me again in that disrespectful way. Do you understand? You have a choice. Are you listening? Good. If you choose to speak to me in a disrespectful way again, you will not be allowed to play on the trampoline for a whole day."

Take away any privilege or activity that he enjoys, and make sure you can actually enforce the punishment. Be firm and unsmiling. Check for understanding. "Do you understand what your choice is, Coltan?" If he seems unsure, repeat it and make sure that he understands how he is supposed to act when you leave for work. Say, "Coltan, when Mommy leaves for work, I expect you to say 'Goodbye, Mommy' in a nice way. You don't have to be happy about me going to work, but you do have to be respectful."

The first time he succeeds in saying goodbye in a respectful manner, reward him with a hug and tell him how proud you are of what a respectful, kind person he is. Give him positive feedback every time he speaks to you in the new, respectful manner, but if he chooses to speak disrespect-fully, back up your threat—follow through. You must say what you mean and mean what you say.

Scenario 7—Don't Be Swayed By Hysterics

If you are concerned about the emotion your child is expressing as you are disciplining him, you will not be an effective parent. You have to be strong enough in your own stance and know that what you are doing is correct in order to effectively continue the discipline. Your child can act whatever way he wants, but it won't sway you. You have to spot the manipulation.

Negotiation is fine once in a while, but when it comes to the kid manipulating: "You can con me once; you can con me twice. But if you con me three times, then I'm stupid."

A typical situation would be a teenaged girl who has been told that she cannot attend a party with friends. You know there will be alcohol and drugs at the party, although she denies or downplays it. You are also not crazy about the friends she plans to go with, and you especially don't like the fact that older guys seem to be interested in her. In addition, the parents who own the party house have a reputation for going away for the weekend and allowing parties.

You have a million reasons to say "no," but your daughter thinks you are being unfair. She says you don't trust her. Then the waterworks start, and she shouts at you through tears that you don't love her, you never let her have any fun, you hate her friends, and you want her to be an unpopu-lar geek. [*Let me just interrupt here, in case you didn't already know: A great deal of illegal drug use and sexual activity occur at teen parties. Last year, a student from my school overdosed and died at a teen party.*]

Here's what you do:

- Allow her to rant to a degree. However, your only responses should be foggers: "Uh-huh," or "I understand," or just plain silence if you are getting angry.
- If you feel so angry that you're afraid of blowing it, just walk away. When both of you have calmed down, resume the discussion.
- Decide what you will repeat as a broken record. She thinks you don't trust her. Say that you *do* trust her, but you don't necessarily trust everybody at the party. When she says, "You hate my friends," be a broken record: "I trust you, honey, but

I don't necessarily trust everyone at the party." When she says, "You never let me have fun!" be a broken record, "I want you to have fun, honey, but I don't necessarily trust everybody at the party."

- Do not allow her to corner you. You're in charge; you're the adult. If you need to remind her of that, ask, "Who's your mother?"

- Remind her that, even if she stays clean during the party, she could be in a lot of trouble if it is busted by the police. ("I can't allow you to do anything that is not in your best interest or mine.")

- If she defies you and goes to the party, you will have to take away privileges and be very strict about the follow through. However, most kids will not get to this point. Most kids will grudgingly obey.

- If you have a mostly trusting relationship, your daughter will eventually see that you felt strongly enough to protect her from going to this party, and maybe for good reason.

Scenario 8—Tough Love for the Pot-smoking, Truant Son

I was doing a parent workshop in the Southwest and had about three hundred people in the audience. After about thirty minutes, I was interrupted by a man who was sitting in the back of the room—he was about 6'2", had a thin build, and had on a flannel shirt and a pair of Levis. He waved at me, and I said, "Sir, you have a question?"

"Well," he said. "I've got a fifteen-year-old kid who smokes dope on the front porch and won't go to school. How ya gonna fix that?"

This is a typical statement on the part of a frustrated parent.

My comment was to him, "Sir, are you ready to hear the answer?"

"Well, yeah, that's why I asked the question."

"I'm going to give you an answer. Do you want to hear it?"

"Yes."

"All right. There are two pieces to it. Number one: accept the fact that you have not done a good job with your son for the first fifteen years of his life because he is totally disrespecting you by smoking dope on the front porch of your house and by not going to school. Number two: if you want to stop what is going on, you take your kid out of school for home schooling. You essentially 'handcuff' your kid to you for the next twelve months. Now what do you do for a living?"

"I'm a drywaller."

"Perfect. Teach your kid how to drywall in the next twelve months. But the thing you must understand is this: Your child totally disrespects you, so you have to use the tough love technique in order to get this thing turned around. Don't you ever for the next twelve months let that boy out of your sight. You don't go anywhere without him, and he doesn't go anywhere without you."

The man looked at me and said, "Well, I don't know if I can do that."

"Then you weren't ready for the answer."

I went on with my presentation. At the end, the man came up to me when everybody else was gone. He was a little humble and he said, "Sir, when you gave me that answer, did you mean it?"

"Yes, I was very, very straight with you."

He said, "I'm going to do it."

"Go to it," I encouraged him. "And I'm going to be coming back on some business. I'll tell you when I'm here, and we can talk."

To make the story short, he did it. He pulled his kid out of school, put him on home school, and he shaped the kid up. But you understand he had to do it with tough love. He also taught his kid how to drywall. He taught his kid that he was in charge of the whole operation.

See, if you don't pay your dues now, you're going to pay them later, and that's what happened with this father. He did not pay his dues early, so he had this "animal" that co-habited on the premises, doing whatever it wanted to do. The father had to become proactive, get tough, and show how much he cared about his kid in order to turn things around.

Scenario 9—Tough Love for the Drug User in a Blended Family

When we met Peg and Jim they had been married about six months. Each of them brought two teenagers into the family. One of the fourteen-year-olds, Peg's son, got into drugs—smoking marijuana and things like that. They came to us and said, "What do we do?"

"You've got to keep very close tabs on your son," I said. "So I recommend that you go to school and you talk to one of the assistant principals and tell him exactly what the situation is. This is so the assistant principal keeps an eye on your son during the course of the school day. You will then bring that boy to school in the morning, walk him in to the assistant principal's office, and turn him over to the assistant principal. The assistant principal, using what we call a sheltering technique, will see that he is taken to classes (because the kid was running away from school).

Then you pick him up after school. This way, while he's at school, he's really going to school. But from the time you pick him up after school to the time he goes back to school the next morning, he's with you constantly. Don't let the boy out of your sight. Do this for one year, and you'll save your son."

Well, Jim and Peg told us the story of their first anniversary. Jim took Peg out to a nice restaurant. He looked across the table at Peg and said, "Peggy, I love you very much."

Peg looked back and said, "Jim, I love you very much."

Then both of them turned to their son and said, "We love you very much, too"—he really was going every place with them at that point.

Scenario 10—Teach Your Child How to Behave in a Store

Children need to be explicitly taught how to behave in many social situations. This kind of training needs to begin when they're very young. When a parent realizes that a youngster is getting into a begging routine in a store, it's just like any behavior: You have to teach the behavior that you want.

An example of this would be a shopping trip with your three-year-old. As you're driving to the grocery store, you say to your three-year-old, "Now, son, we're going to go into the store, and we're going to go shopping, and I'm going to put you into the shopping cart, and you are not to beg for things. You are not to ask me for candy or any other thing. If you choose to do that, then I'm going to stop the cart where it is, and you and I are going to come right back out to the car. We'll sit in the car for five minutes. At the end of five minutes, we'll go back into the store." Then you might have the youngster repeat what you said, just for clarity. The repeating doesn't do the real job, though, because the child hasn't internalized it yet.

The key is, when you get into the store, and you're walking around and the child says, "Mommy, I want that candy bar!" You don't even say anything. You just stop, take the child out of the cart, and you walk to the car. You put the child in the back seat, and you sit in the front seat. Then you say, "Jeremy, when five minutes are up, we're going to go back into the grocery store. You understand why Mommy brought you out here. You are not to ask for things." Now, at that point, the child may comply with you or the child may not comply. If the child complies, he will sit there and sulk. If he doesn't comply, he'll begin to cry and manipulate. They will say things like, "I'll never do it again," "I'm sorry," or "You don't love me," but you are to ignore all that. Do not respond to the child's behavior in that regard. Simply wait for the "five minutes" to be up, and, please remember, parents, that little kids cannot tell time. When a minute's up, that's usually long enough. When the time is up just say, "Okay, that's five minutes. We're going to go back into the store." Look the kid in the eye as you're getting him out of the car seat and say, "Remember, you are not to beg me for candy bars or toys or anything else." Then you go back into the store, put the child in the shopping cart, and you begin your shopping again. If the child begs for something again, you stop and go through the routine again.

Now, the point here is that this shopping trip is not necessarily about getting groceries; this shopping event is to teach your child how to go shopping. That's what it's all about. It may take you an extra hour, but that extra hour is going to pay you dividends. So, say what you mean, mean what you say, and never say anything that you cannot back up.

The same approach applies to tantrums.

Scenario 11—Tantrums and Other Anti-social Behavior

When a child throws a tantrum, it is because he expects you to give him something; he wants you to do something or provide something for him, but it's also more complicated than that. If you have a kid who is yelling and kicking and screaming at the age of two, that means that you, the parent, have lost a lot of battles up to then because children learn behavior. If they learn that anti-social behavior is appropriate and works for them, they'll use it. That's manipulation. So if your two-year-old is out of control, you just have to say to yourself, "I haven't been firm with my child to this point. I'm going to start it now."

When your child throws a tantrum in a store or any other public place, tell him that you're going back to the car because of his behavior. When he resists you say, "When I say I'm going to take you back out to the car, you're going to the car. If I have to drag you, you're going to the car." You pick your two-year-old up, and you might walk out or you might stop to look at a toy on the way as a way to distract him, but you're not going to cave in to the manipulative demands of the child. This child has to learn moderation. He has to learn the discipline required to be in a place like that. The key here is giving the child specific directions for an activity, even if he's two years old. He has a brain, but his attention span is shorter, so your patience will have to be greater.

Of course, there are other types of anti-social behavior. If your child is hitting the cat, scratching the tabletop, or fighting with her cousin, that has to stop. You have to pay attention and not let it happen. Pick your child up, hold her close to you and say, "You're not to do that." Give your child directions. She must hear directions from you in terms of her behavior. For instance, you might say, "Angela, when we walk into the store, you are to walk beside me. You are not to wander off." Then you quiz her: "What do you do when we go into the store, Angela?"

"Walk beside you, Daddy."

So the purpose is to communicate your expectations. You teach, remind, and hover—and by *hover* I mean: you watch, you watch, you watch because you care.

Note from Mary: Most parents of young children believe that if you discipline your children in public—or don't discipline them—you're judged negatively either way. But, as Bert explained above, there is a better way to approach taking the small ones out in public, and it includes a plan. A day before transcribing these scenarios, I was in a Fred Meyer store and heard a child giving his mother a hard time. I heard them before I saw them. The little blond boy looked to be about two and was trying to stand up and get out of the shopping cart. The mother was cajoling and begging him to sit and cooperate, but the little boy just kept struggling with her. They rounded a corner, and a second later I heard what I knew I'd hear—the howl and then the screaming, which continued until I got myself out of earshot because temper tantrums are very uncomfortable for me, as they are for all shoppers. I know you have all witnessed this a thousand times.

What the mother should have done is talk to her son about her expectations before they went in the store. She should have said, "Andy, when we're in the store, you will sit in the cart and help Mommy shop for as long as I need you to. If you choose to get up out of the cart, if you cry or scream, we will come right back to the car." With a two-year-old it is wise, of course, to make sure the child has eaten before you shop, that her diaper is clean, and that she is not in need of a nap. But a child of this age can be trained just like a three- or four-year-old. It may take an hour or two out of your day, and you may have to repeat the lesson more often than with an older child. But let's look at it this way: You can always go to the grocery store. Raising your child, on the other hand, is the most important thing you will ever do, and doing it well takes foresight and technique.

Appendix B:
Essential Concepts

PARENTING PLAN (PRENUPTIAL)

The problem with most parents is that they do not think ahead. Most couples do not have a parenting plan, for instance, when they plan to marry. Bert tells this story of one such couple:

> I recently went out to dinner with a wonderful couple who is engaged to be married. He is a high school principal, and she teaches elementary school. The young lady—I'll call her Jennifer—looked at me at one point and said, "Mr. Simmons, you know that Matthew and I are getting married in June. Would you give us some advice?"
>
> I said, "Yes, I can give you a piece of advice. Are you planning on having children?"
>
> "Yes" she said.
>
> Matthew chimed in and said, "I'd like to have about five."
>
> Jennifer smiled, and I said, "You have to talk about how you're going to raise them. Matthew has to tell you what he thinks, and you've got to tell Matthew what you think because if you don't, you'll have conflict."

Matthew and Jennifer are typical in that they hadn't talked about how they planned to raise their children. Unless a husband and wife take part in premarital counseling or something similar, they normally do not discuss child-rearing. Yet addressing, together, how you will raise children prior to marriage is responsible and proactive and worthy of the most important job in the world. Here are some issues to address in a parenting plan:

1. What kind of discipline will we use? Be specific. (Examples: Is spanking okay or not? Time-outs? Grounding? Taking away privileges?)
2. What are our goals as parents? What kind of values do we want to instill in our children? (Examples: How will our children learn

manners? How will they be allowed to speak to people? Will swearing of any kind be allowed in the household? What is our stance on alcohol and drug consumption?)

3. How will we approach the issue of school and achievement? What are our expectations? (Examples: What are good enough grades? Will our children be expected to go to college? How will we pay for it?)

4. What kind of religious or spiritual education, if any, will we provide for our child? (Example: If the spouses were raised with different religions, how will this be resolved with the children?)

5. How will we spend holidays, and with whom?

6. What is good nutrition, and how can we instill healthful habits in our children? (Examples: How much TV a day is okay? How much exercise should our kids get?)

Add any other issues to this list that you think are relevant. Type up your agreed responses, date it, and put it in a safe place.

Nonassertive and Hostile Parents vs. Assertive and Proactive Parents

Nonassertive and Hostile

Most people are habitually nonassertive which usually culminates in hostility. This can produce domestic violence, for instance. This kind of emotional and physical violence results from a combination of nonassertive behavior (not acting), allowing a negative situation to go on and on, and then reacting with anger and hostility at a later point. People who don't know how to handle anger become hostile.

Here are some common traits of nonassertive and hostile parents:

- Get their needs met through fear
- Yell
- Scream
- Threaten
- Blame
- Give up on their kids
- Are inconsistent
- Have no plan

Reactive parents do not plan how to work with serious misbehavior. This is why frustration becomes the result of the parent-child relationship.

Reactive parents are not consistent, do not follow through, and gain no positive results.

Assertive and Proactive

Proactive, assertive people think ahead. They plan. They conduct themselves in an assertive manner, meaning they get their needs met, but they don't do it at the expense of others. They are firm, fair, and consistent. If you are an assertive person, you get your needs met as a parent in appropriate ways that are uncharacteristic of most of the population.

Here are some common traits of assertive and proactive parents:

- Get their needs met by using skills, being consistent, and following through
- Have a plan (with steps) how to work successfully with serious misbehavior: 1-2-3-4-5-6 . . . "This is what I am going to do."
- Persist: "I am not going away."
- Get assistance from teachers, counselors, and administrators
- Follow their plan!

LOOKING FAIR AND SOUNDING FAIR

"Looking Fair" means facing your child and making eye contact, but not necessarily smiling. Nod and agree when you can. Show your concern. If compromise is an option, that can be discussed. Do not argue. Be a "broken record" or use foggers if necessary.

Sounding fair means using the word *choice*. Tell your child, "You have a choice. If you continue to argue with me, you won't be driving the car at all. I am concerned about your safety, and my decision stands." This is the end of the conversation.

The parent needs to know the discussion is over at this point. The child—if there is a history of trust and consistency in the relationship—will abide by the parent's decision without a lot of fuss. He may complain (to himself) momentarily, but that is to save face, and he will settle into the caring adult's decision, like it or not.

WHAT TO DO WITH SUDDEN ANGER: WALKING AWAY, "I" STATEMENTS, AND PARADOXICAL RESPONSES

Walking Away

If you are too angry to conduct yourself in a civil manner, tell your child that you must calm down and walk away. Come back to the discussion at hand with your child when both of you have calmed down.

"I" Statements

This is not an original technique. Many have used it to their advantage. When you are angry:

- **Describe what you see**: Use "I" statements. "I see a pile of laundry that I asked you to do yesterday, and I see a lot homework that has not been done." "I see grades on this progress report that are not acceptable." "I see someone standing here who said she would be here a half hour ago."
- **Describe what you feel**: "I feel very angry and disappointed." "I feel like you don't value your education or take me seriously." "When you don't show up when you say you will, I get worried, and it also puts me in an uncomfortable position with others."
- **Describe what needs to be done**: "This laundry must be done today."—"Your homework must be done before you do anything else."—"It's important that you are a person of your word. That means following through on what you say you'll do."

Paradoxical Responses

You do the exact opposite of what is expected. The natural reaction to anger is for the tummy to tighten and the face to show anger and pain. Become conscious of how you look and feel. This takes control but will come with practice. Here's what you do:

- Let your tummy relax.
- Give a look of assurance, a look of quietness, a thoughtful look.
- Let your brain take over the gut reaction. Back off, slow down.
- Lower your voice or don't talk at all.
- You may even walk away and address the issue later when you are calm.

BREAKING UP THE FIGHT BETWEEN SIBLINGS:
CHOOSING ONE KID

When children fight, one mistake parents make is trying to find out who caused it. Tell your kids that the next time something goes on between them, you will just pick somebody and discipline them, "I'm just picking one because I know both of you are involved." So Jimmy and Johnny get in a fight, and the parent says, "Come with me, Jimmy."

"Well, he hit me first!" But you just take one. You aren't taking one kid's word over another. That's being fair! Parents want to be fair and nice and listen to all the particulars, but that's a waste of time when your goal is to have the fighting stop, period. You know it will all flush out in the end.

"What are you going to do with me?" the child will ask.

"You're going to follow me around for the next three hours."

Then make sure that what you do for the next three hours is really dull for the kid. If you can remember which one you chose last night, choose the other one next time, but don't worry too much about it.

THE SCHOOL AND HOME PLAN:
PRIORITIZING AND REVOKING PRIVILEGES

- Determine desired behaviors.
- Teach the desired behaviors.
- Remind the child of the behaviors—often.
- Be attentive and observant.
- Use positive re-enforcers (incentives, rewards).
- Make a Plan: Determine those activities the child enjoys in priority order (see examples below):

Elementary School Age
1. TV
2. Bike
3. Friends
4. Video games
5. Bedtime (go to bed an hour earlier than usual)

Secondary School Age
1. Cell phone
2. Car
3. Computer
4. TV
5. Friends

If it becomes necessary to involve a school official with your child's discipline plan (if there are attendance or behavior problems at school), do the following as well:

- Inform the school official of your discipline plan and describe their part in it (walk the child to class, meet briefly with child every morning, and so forth).
- Check in with the school official (teacher or administrator) to see how things went each day.

Enforce punishments for misbehavior by taking away one item each day and (for elementary students) going to bed an hour early. Positive behavior should result in all privileges being available as usual.

POST THE HOUSE RULES

Rules are usually spoken, but it doesn't hurt to write them down and post them on the refrigerator. Example for an eight-year-old:

Ryan
1. Put your bats and balls away after practice.
2. Have homework done by 7:30 so you can watch some TV.
3. The ratio of reading to video game play must be equal.
4. Use an indoor voice with your little sister.
5. No running in the house when your friends are over.

PROVIDE POSITIVE SUPPORT

With the twelve and under crowd, praise them and their success. With teenagers, praise what they have done, the products of their success, not them as people. (Teens tend to feel judged with both positive and negative feedback.) Facilitate intrinsic rewards (positive internal feelings of accomplishment and self-esteem) and not material rewards. Aim for the inner and not the outer.

Non-verbal Praise:
Wink
Thumbs Up
"High 5"
Smile
Nod
Pat on Shoulder
Special Handshake
Hug

Follow a cycle of positive re-enforcement: Always give three positives for every negative: one negative ☹, three positives ☺ ☺ ☺—always.

Appendix C: The Full List

If an "M" is listed after a commandment, it means the commandment was written by a male. If an "F" is listed, the commandment was written by a female. Commandments with asterisks were written by groups of students and not exclusive to one gender.

What Kids Don't Want:
NAGGING, YELLING, PUNISHMENT, ABUSE
(NONASSERTIVE, HOSTILE PARENTING)

1. Not getting on me about things that are *my* problems. (F)
2. Don't tell me to do things on my own then get mad when they come out wrong. (F)
3. Don't sound so happy when you wake me up at 6 am. (M)
4. A parent should not be hypercritical in their punishments. (M)
5. A parent should never abuse their children. (M)
6. Do not abuse or mistreat your children in any way. (F)
7. Thou shalt not punish in an abusive manner. (F)
8. Thou shall not force school work upon thy child. (F)
9. No yelling. (M)
10. No nagging. (M)
11. No grounding. (M)
12. Thou shalt have a real reason for refusal. (No "Because I'm your parent") (M)
13. Thou shall not punish me for small reasons. (M)
14. Don't make up punishments randomly. (M)
15. Keep things in proportion (don't make small things a big deal). (M)

16. Thou shall not verbally or physically abuse thy youth. (M)
17. Thou shall not scold me in a time of need. (F)
18. Thou shalt not kill. (F)
19. Thou shall not revoke phone usage. (M)
20. Thou shall not force hygiene. (M)
21. Thou shalt not revoke school privileges. (M)
22. Thou shalt not revoke sports activities. (M)
23. Thou shall not pester me about working or anything job-related. (M)
24. Don't yell. (F)
25. No beating kids. (M)
26. Don't physically or mentally abuse your child. (F)
27. Thou shall watch thy tongue. Harmful words may stay long after you have forgotten them.
28. Thou shall not fight with thy child. (M)
29. Thou shall not try to turn a child against the other parent. (M)
30. Don't provoke your child to wrath. (M)
31. Don't abuse them. (M)
32. Don't harass them. (M)
33. Thou shall not take away my license/keys for every little thing I do wrong. (M)
34. Don't take it out on me when you have a bad day. (F)
35. Thou shall not give unreasonable punishments. (M)
36. Do not accuse your children of things before asking their side of the story. (F)
37. Do not make rules without understandable reasons for them. (F)
38. Don't abuse your children. (M)
39. Don't abuse your position of power. (M)
40. Thou shall not abuse thy children. (M)
41. Thou shall not abuse thy parental power. (M)
42. No hitting a child. (F)
43. No abusive punishments. (F)
44. No excessive yelling at children. (F)
45. * Overreacting doesn't help the situation.
46. * Thou shalt not nag.
47. * Thou shalt not yell at me.

48.   * Thou shalt not punish me for long periods of time.
49.   * Thou shalt not criticize me.
50.   * Thou shalt not ground us.
51.   * Procrastination is not a sin.
52.   * Thou shall not ask incriminating questions.
53.   * Thou shalt not be strict.
54.   * Thou shalt not hit me.
55.   * Thou shalt not yell at me.
56.   * Thou shalt not lose your temper.
57.   * Thou shalt not yell if we can't yell back.
58.   * Thou shalt not ground me.
59.   * Thou shalt not raise they voice in my kingdom.
60.   * Thou shalt not abuse.
61.   * Thou shalt not raise your voice in anger toward human beings.
62.   * Thou shalt not be stubborn.
63.   * Thou shalt not ground me.
64.   * Thou shalt not withhold my money.
65.   * Thou shalt not blackmail me.
66.   * Thou shalt not hassle me about daily issues.
67.   * Don't overreact.
68.   * Don't force your kids to do something they don't want to do.
69.   * Thou shalt not argue with your kids.
70.   * Thou shalt not banish kids to their rooms.
71.   * Thou should not hit your kids.
72.   * Thou shalt not ground us.
73.   * Thou shalt not hit your kids.
74.   * Thou shalt not threaten to take away the car.
75.   * Thou shalt not abuse your power.
76.   * Thou shalt not hold me to double standards.
77.   * Thou shall not get angry when your child gets a ticket and thou shall pay for the ticket.
78.   * Thou shall never take a loud tone with thy offspring.
79.   * Thou shan't kill thy offspring.
80.   * Thou shall not abuse children.
81.   * No yelling.
82.   * Don't abuse power.

83.　* Thou shall not abuse they child.

84.　* Thou shall not abuse thy power.

85.　* Thou shalt not provoke thine children to wrath.

86.　* Thou shalt not punish thine child.

87.　* Thou shall not beat me or I will kill you.

88.　* Thou shalt not ground me.

89.　* Thou shalt not take away my license.

90.　* Thou shalt stop backseat driving.

100.　* Thou shalt not raise thy voice to me.

101.　* Thou shalt not use my full name in anger.

102.　* Thou shalt not verbally or physically abuse thy youth.

103.　* Thou shalt not make stupid rules.

104.　* Thou shalt not punish in an abusive manner.

105.　* Thou shall not ground us.

106.　* Thou shalt not beat children profusely.

107.　* Thou shall not strike unless stricken.

108.　* Thou shall not ground.

109.　* Thou shall not swear at thine children.

110.　* Don't give unfair punishments.

111.　* Thou shalt not raise thy voice in anger.

112.　* Thou shalt not ground your child.

113.　* Thou shalt not kill or hurt.

114.　* Thou shalt not abuse.

115.　* Thou shalt not put down your children.

116.　* Thou shalt not yell at thy children.

117.　* Thou shall not yell.

118.　* Don't yell at your kids.

119.　* Thou shall not nag.

120.　* Thou shall not falsely accuse.

121.　* Have understandable reasons for your rules.

122.　* Thou shalt not scream and yell in my face when you get angry.

123.　* Thou shalt not nag.

124.　* Thou shalt not yell.

125.　* Thou shalt not nag.

126.　* You will not punish without reason.

127.　* You won't ground me or give me a curfew if I am a good kid and call you periodically.

128. * Thou shalt not be irrational when punishing.
129. * Thou shalt not beat your child.
130. * Thou shall not abuse, physically or emotionally.
131. * Thou shall not use any form of abuse.
132. * Thou shalt not holler at kids.
133. * Thou shalt not punish.
134. * Thou shalt not complain.
135. Thou shall never take a tone not needed. (M)
136. Thou shall never hit. (M)
137. Thou shall not raise thy voice in anger. (F)
138. Thou shall not raise they hand in anger. (F)
139. Thou shall not abuse. (F)
140. Thou shall not harm me. (M)
141. Thou shall not over discipline your child. (M)
142. Don't take out your anger at others on me. (M)
143. Don't yell at me like I am not old enough to understand. (M)
144. Thou shall not over-punish a child. (M)
145. Ye shall not over-punish me. (F)
146. Thou shall not get too mad over the mistakes we make—it happens. (F)
147. Thou shalt never strike thine own children. (M)
148. Let it go! (F)
149. Do NOT STRIKE or abuse. (M)
150. Let it go. (M)
151. Thou shall not abuse your position. (F)
152. Thou shall never hit your children. (F)
153. Thou shall never disown thy children. (F)
154. Thou shall not be so anal about the littlest things. (M)
155. Don't hold grudges against them and not speak to them. (F)
156. Do not yell; it does not help anyone. (F)
157. Do not physically touch (in anger) or harm your children in any way. (F)
158. Let it go! (F)
159. Thou shall try really hard not to make thy children's life so hard. (F)
160. Thou shall not abuse verbally or physically. (F)
161. You will not beat or abuse your child in any way. (F)
162. You will not judge or punish your child irrationally. (F)

163. Thou shall not strike thy children. (F)
164. Thou shall not ground me. (F)
165. Realize that grounding kids doesn't help. (M)
166. Thou shall not abuse your children. (M)
167. Thou shall not be hypercritical. (F)
168. Thou shall not be abusive. (F)
169. Thou shall not yell for it solves nothing. (F)
170. Parents will stop talking when children say enough. (M)
171. Parents shalt not lecture past 10 minutes in one sitting. (M)
172. Thou shall not be abusive. (M)
173. Thou shalt never assume something is wrong. (F)
174. Thou shall not be cruel. (M)
175. Thou shall not get mad. (M)
176. Thou shall never raise your voice at me. (F)
177. * LET IT GO!
178. * Thou shall never hit.
179. * Thou shall know that yelling doesn't get your point across.
180. * Thou shall not beat thy children.
181. * Thou shall not abuse your children.
182. * Thou shalt never raise they voice in anger.
183. * Don't physically or verbally abuse your children.
184. * Thou shall not be spiteful.
185. * Thou shall not turn to the Dark Side.
186. * Thou shall not hit or strike.
187. * Don't be mean.
188. * When you're angry at others, don't take it out on me.
189. * Thou shall not freak out.
190. * Thou shall not bitch!
191. * Thou shall not yell.
192. * Thou shall not abuse your child.
193. * Thou shall control your temper.
194. * Thou shall not overpunish.

What Kids Do Want:

DISCIPLINE, PATIENCE, EMPATHY, UNDERSTANDING
(ASSERTIVE, PROACTIVE PARENTING)

1. Enforce rules upon children. (M)
2. Thou shall be fair. (F)
3. Thou shall compromise. (F)
4. Thou shalt hold me accountable. (M)
5. Thou shall give justice to those who deserve it. (M)
6. Choose your battles. (M)
7. Be flexible with rules. (F)
8. Hold me responsible for my actions. (M)
9. Have real reasons for rules. (M)
10. Don't be too strict. (F)
11. Thou shall yell at me and keep me in line. (M)
12. Use tough love. (M)
13. Thou shalt not tolerate disrespectful arguing. (M)
14. School shalt come first, friends and family second, everything else shall come last. (M)
15. Set rules and boundaries. (F)
16. Be fair whenever possible. (F)
17. Talking something out works better than grounding. (F)
18. * Set reasonable expectations.
19. * Thou shalt not ground for more than 2 days.
20. * Thou shalt not be strict.
21. * Thou shalt not be strict.
22. * Thou shalt hold me accountable for my actions.
23. * Thou shalt always have a real reason.
24. * Thou shall make sure we don't get out of line.
25. * Thou shalt reward thy child when doing good.
26. * Be flexible with rules.
27. * Thou shalt not push child too hard.
28. * Thou shall be reasonable.
29. * Thou shall have patience and not yell.
30. * Thou shalt be flexible.
31. * Thou shalt be reasonable.
32. Forgive
33. * Thou shalt forgive and forget thy children.

34.   * Thou shalt forgive instead of punish.

35.   * Thou shalt forgive a child for his/her mistakes.

36.   * Thou shalt have good reasoning behind decisions.

37.   * Give kids a chance to explain what happened.

38.   * Thou shalt forgive.

39.   * Thou shall think of disciplining as teaching, not punishment.

40.   * Thou shalt be reasonable (moms).

41.   * Thou shalt give us a chance to explain.

42.   Never give up on your children. (M)

43.   Be understanding. (F)

44.   Try to remember what it was like being a teenager. (F)

45.   Thou shalt think before thou acts. (M)

46.   * Thou shalt put yourself in my shoes.

47.   * Be understanding.

48.   * Thou shalt be understanding.

49.   * Be understanding.

50.   * Be understanding.

51.   * Thou shalt be understanding.

52.   * Thou shalt be patient and understanding.

53.   * Thou shalt be understanding.

54.   * Be understanding with mistakes.

55.   * Thou shall be patient, kind, and understanding.

56.   * Thou shall understand my needs and wants.

57.   * Thou shall remember being young.

58.   Thou shall keep me in line when needed. (M)

59.   Thou shall forgive. (M)

60.   Thou shall scold. (F)

61.   Thou shall force children to attend school. (M)

62.   Thou shall set limits and boundaries for me. (F)

63.   Thou shall make consequences when necessary. (F)

64.   Thou shall deal punishment fairly. (F)

65.   Thou shalt not jump to conclusions. (M)

66.   You shall set fair consequences for misbehavior. (M)

67.   Thou shall keep children in school. (M)

68.   Thou shall punish me minimally and accordingly. (F)

69.   Advise, don't criticize. (M)

70.   Discipline your child and show responsibility. (M)

71. Give me the benefit of the doubt; after all, I am your child. (M)
72. Be forgiving of my mistakes, because I have learned from them, even if you don't think I have. (M)
73. Refrain from long, drawn out lectures. Instead, wait until a later time to discuss the problem in a positive way. The end result: no yelling and a lesson learned. (M)
74. Thou shall treat your children fairly. (M)
75. Thou shall keep fair and consistent rules. (M)
76. Thou shall give us consequences for our negligent or irresponsible behavior. (F)
77. Thou shall forgive. (F)
78. Set reasonable boundaries and restrictions. (M)
79. Don't be quick to judge. (M)
80. Be open minded. (M)
81. Be patient. (M)
82. Thou shall set reasonable limitations, which can be changed as our age does. (F)
83. Enforce appropriate discipline toward your child. (F)
84. Punish when needed. (M)
85. Have reasonable discipline. (F)
86. Relax. (M)
87. Assess situation before yelling. (M)
88. Thou shall agree to disagree. (F)
89. Thou shall set rules. (M)
90. Thou shall set limits. (F)
91. Thou shall be good disciplinarian and understanding friend. (F)
92. Thou shall discipline. (M)
93. Thou shall be reasonable. (F)
94. Verbal abuse only, but not too harsh. (F)
95. Thou shall be reasonable. (F)
96. Thou shall only discipline with verbal choices. (F)
97. Give reasonable discipline. (F)
98. Use discipline but not physical. (M)
99. Talk through problems, not yell. (M)
100. Set boundaries but not in stone . . . you should grow and learn as does your child. (F)

101. Be firm but not mean. (M)
102. Make rules the same for all kids in the household. (F)
103. Set boundaries. (F)
104. Thou shall set standards of behavior. (F)
105. Thou shall forgive and forget mistakes. (F)
106. Try to understand them. (M)
107. Thou shall discipline me. (F)
108. Thou shall give me a reason for your answer. (F)
109. Thou shall understand that people make mistakes. (F)
110. Remember you were a kid once, so have an open mind. (M)
111. Thou shall forgive your kids. (M)
112. Set limits. (M)
113. Thou shall set boundaries. (M)
114. Thou shall teach me discipline. (F)
115. * Set limits.
116. * Thou shall set boundaries for thy children.
117. * Thou shall discipline and teach.
118. * Give reasonable discipline.
119. * Praise child.
120. * Thou shall only set rules when needed.
121. * Only verbal punishments.
122. * Thou shall be reasonable.
123. * Thou shall teach me discipline.
124. * Thou shall set rules.
125. * Thou shall give discipline.
126. * Thou shall make us abide by your reasonable limitations.
127. * Thou shall refrain from giving too much discipline.
128. * Punish them when needed.
129. * Be forgiving.
130. * Let them make mistakes but don't let them repeat them.
131. * Thou shall learn to forgive.
132. * Thou shall understand.
133. * Thou shall forgive.
134. * Thou shall expect responsibility. (from kids)

About the Author

Mary teaches high school in Bothell, Washington, where she has lived for twenty years. Born in Oregon, Mary was raised with her two brothers and sister in the Willamette Valley by parents who were teachers. She fell in love with literature while attending Southern Oregon University, and pursued her MA at the University of Victoria in Canada. Mary is blessed with a wonderful family and a close circle of friends and colleagues. She is the mother of one son of whom she is inordinately proud.

Her father, Bert Simmons, with whom she wrote this book, went on to be a high school principal after teaching. He is now an educational consultant with his own business: Simmons Associates, The Education Company.